Moreton Morrell Site

KT-599-907

WITHDRAWN

Ethics in the Workplace

Warwickshire College

00677030

WITHDRAWN

Ethics in the Workplace
A Systems Perspective

William F. Roth

DeSales University

WARWICKSHIRE
COLLEGE
LIBRARY

PEARSON

Prentice
Hall

Upper Saddle River, New Jersey 07458

Library of Congress Cataloging-in-Publication Data

Roth, William F.
   Ethics in the workplace: a systems perspective / by William F. Roth—1st ed.
    p. cm.
   Includes bibliographical references and index.
   ISBN 0-13-184815-1
   1. Business ethics. I. Title.

HF5387.R674 2005
174—dc21
                                   2003056338

Editorial Director: Charlyce Jones-Owen
Senior Acquisitions Editor: Ross Miller
Assistant Editor: Wendy Yurash
Editorial Assistant: Carla Worner
Director of Marketing: Beth Gillette-Mejia
Senior Marketing Assistant: Jennifer Bryant
Production Liaison: Joanne Hakim
Manufacturing Buyer: Christina Helder
Cover Art Director: Jayne Conte
Cover Design: Bruce Kenselaar
Cover Image Specialist: Karen Sanatar
Cover Illustration/Photo: Photodisc Collection/Getty Images, Inc.
Composition/Full-Service Project Management: Fran Daniele/Preparé Inc.
Printer/Binder: Courier Printing Companies

WARWICKSHIRE COLLEGE
LIBRARY

Class No
1744 ROT

Acc No
00677030

Price & Loan Type
18.99 Loan

Credits and acknowledgments borrowed from other sources and reproduced, with permission, in this textbook appear on appropriate page within text.

Copyright © 2005 by Pearson Education, Inc., Upper Saddle River, New Jersey, 07458.
Pearson Prentice Hall. All rights reserved. Printed in the United States of America. This publication is protected by Copyright and permission should be obtained from the publisher prior to any prohibited reproduction, storage in a retrieval system, or transmission in any form or by any means, electronic, mechanical, photocopying, recording, or likewise. For information regarding permission(s), write to: Rights and Permissions Department.

Pearson Prentice Hall™ is a trademark of Pearson Education, Inc.
Pearson® is a registered trademark of Pearson plc
Prentice Hall® is a registered trademark of Pearson Education, Inc.

Pearson Education LTD., London
Pearson Education Singapore, Pte. Ltd
Pearson Education, Canada, Ltd
Pearson Education–Japan
Pearson Education Australia PTY, Limited

Pearson Education North Asia Ltd
Pearson Educación de Mexico, S.A. de C.V.
Pearson Education Malaysia, Pte. Ltd
Pearson Education, Upper Saddle River, New Jersey

PEARSON
Prentice
Hall

10 9 8 7 6 5 4 3 2
ISBN 0-13-184815-1

I dedicate this book to Eric Trist,
my teacher, my friend;
a man who remains for me an ongoing model
for humility and completeness.

With thanks.

Contents

Preface

Ethics in the Workplace: A Systems Perspective delves into the realm of organization ethics. Beginning with a discussion of management characteristics the text uses case studies to demonstrate how most current approaches to improving ethics are seriously flawed, and why they rarely produce, the desired results. If organizations want to improve their ethical climate, the focus should not be on *changing the individual employee*. Rather, it should be on designing organization systems correctly. If this is done, the need or the temptation for employees to behave unethically, will in most cases, disappear.

This book explores the role philosophy and religion have played historically in society's search for the best approach to ethics. The four major schools of ethical thought—utilitarianism, egoism, deontology, and relativism—are outlined and discussed. The book identifies the weaknesses exhibited when each school of thought is put into practice and shows us that a generic standard of ethical criteria is necessary if we are to get beyond the traditional arguments. The book identifies such a standard and shows how it supports each of the four major schools, merging them so that they are no longer contradictory.

At this point *Ethics in the Workplace: A Systems Perspective* introduces the systems approach as the best vehicle for reshaping our workplace culture according to our new standard. The systemic characteristics necessary to the creation of a more ethical environment are discussed with a focus on empowerment. Finally, the systemic designs necessary to the realization of these characteristics in key organization processes—evaluation and reward, training, and teambuilding—are laid out.

Good reading, and take care.

William F. Roth
DeSales University

Acknowledgments

My education in the systems approach is based on the work of many outstanding thinkers. Those who took the lead in my case, however, those who taught me face to face and gradually molded my thinking were members of a small, select group of men gathered together at the University of Pennsylvania Social Systems Sciences Ph.D. program. One of the leaders of that group was Eric Trist, who took me under his wing and got me headed in the right direction. Another was Russell Ackoff, who continued to shape and to hone rough edges until the job was done. I owe them both a great deal.

I am indebted to the following reviewers: Roy Bywaters, Ursinus College; John Pourdehnad, Ackoff Center for Advancement of Systems Approaches.

There is one other acknowledgment concerning *Ethics in the Workplace: A Systems Perspective* that gives me great pleasure. I would like to thank my two sons. Ian, currently the philosopher in our family, helped me understand existentialism and its relevance to the field of ethics. Dane, the younger, helped with the editing. It was good to have them working with me.

Ethics in the Workplace

Chapter 1

Shortcuts To Failure

THE HARD LESSONS

Which comes first, the chicken or the egg? Which comes first, ethical behavior or systems thinking?

Ethical behavior can be found in companies where the management philosophy is not systemic. Many such organizations exist. Most are led by an extremely powerful, visible father figure or by father figures who provide an example and encourage everyone to follow suit. Most such companies also depend on fear of punishment to help discourage unethical behavior. I would relate this characteristic to traditional religions where a paternalistic system of leaders is in place, where a father figure or a hierarchy of father figures defines the standards that everyone else is expected to follow. Emphasis is on encouraging employees to make the "right" decision and to deny the temptation that always exists.

Systems practitioners believe that rather than placing emphasis on fortifying the individual, it should be placed on correctly defining management philosophy and on designing key organization processes in ways that keep temptation from arising. This is because unethical behavior in organizations that have adopted a true and comprehensive systems approach to management is unnecessary. The situations that encourage it in traditional organizations are not present, they have been designed out of existence.

Is this too good to be true? Not really. Proof exists. A growing number of organizations are now run systemically. While they might have adopted this model for a variety of reasons, all are enjoying increased success and fewer ethical breakdowns as a result. The problem is that the number of companies using the systems approach to management remains relatively small. Most have been unwilling to make the leap despite the growing evidence of its value. They like what they hear in terms of the resulting increased profits, the improved morale, and the heightened ethical workforce behavior. They make a point of reading up on it. But when it comes time to put the approach into place, to actually make the necessary changes, they hesitate, or go at it piecemeal, implementing only those parts that feel comfortable. They resist

1

and reshape the essence of the systems change model. They twist the rules to meet their own immediate needs when these rules cannot be twisted, when the situation is all or nothing. Then, when the desired changes do not occur, they say that the model does not work, or that it takes too long to produce results. So they drop it and move on to the next quick fix.

I recently asked a group of fifteen middle managers representing fifteen organizations why their companies' efforts to improve ethics and to modernize procedures were not producing the desired results. The list of answers included the following:

1. Lack of commitment and lack of a believable message from the top
2. No real effort to get buy-in from employees
3. Companies have not stuck to one approach
4. Companies are focused on short-term rather than long-term results, which makes it more difficult *not* to cheat
5. Companies use the threat of punishment as their prime motivator
6. Employees are too busy dealing with intimidation by bosses and fierce in-house competition
7. Old habits are difficult to change
8. Turnover occurs in key process figures with the new ones changing the rules of the game to demonstrate ownership
9. Companies are unwilling to take the necessary "risks"
10. Companies are unwilling to argue with the success previously enjoyed by doing things the old way
11. Companies are unable or unwilling to learn from the success of other companies

Sound familiar? All of the above are common and valid criticisms. But all of the above are also just symptoms; they are not the cause. The cause lies much deeper. It lies in the culture of the organization, in the management system. Also, the "cause" is not just one cause. It is a collection of intertwined, inseparable factors called "producers" that reinforce each other. These producers are so tightly meshed that even if it was of value they could not be separated. Drawing a definitive boundary around their outermost perimeter would be impossible because that perimeter invades every facet of the organization. One would be forced to say that the entire organization is the "producer," which is, in fact, the truth.

In order to truly improve the ethical climate of an organization we have to change the entire organization. We have to change its culture, its mindset, the way employees (on all levels) think. However, organizations have not yet figured this out. Instead, they jump unprepared into efforts to improve ethics and organization performance, over-complicating the process, over-simplifying it, fragmenting it, customizing it to death, faking it, and spending frightening amounts of money to do so.

We have all heard that successful organization transitions involve cultural change. We nod our heads "yes." Yet we don't really understand. In truth, we don't really want to understand. In most cases understanding would present an overwhelming challenge and we are already overwhelmed. So we fudge it. We go through the motions. We do make some changes but they are isolated, more superficial than foundational. We paint the room a lighter shade of blue to make it appear bigger rather than actually knocking a wall out. And we get away with it, at least in the short run, because our peers are not interested in knocking out walls either.

In the meantime, frustration levels in all segments of the workforce continue to rise as the company is forced by market conditions to focus increasingly on the numbers and decreasingly on the human side—the ethical side of the equation. Management experts say that empowerment, sharing information, and decision-making authority lead to improved ethics, but we follow our gut instinct instead. We tighten controls and spell out ethical requirements more specifically. We depend increasingly on threat and punishment to improve the situation.

And the problem starts at the top.

THE SOURCE

As an advocate of the systems approach I find it interesting that most companies periodically require lower-level employees to sit through ethics training. However, I have also observed that the real problems do not originate with these workers. Rather, most of the real ethical problems originate further up the hierarchy. Has the reader ever heard of an executive corps being required to attend ethics training? I haven't. Anyway, it would be a waste of time. Usually the problem is not with individual executives. Rather, the problem is with the management philosophy they are weaned on or with the management processes they have designed.

Executives and other managers do not warp this philosophy and these systems intentionally. Rather they frequently do not understand the ethical implications of design decisions. Or they *do* understand the implications, they know the effect these decisions will have on the activities of employees but cannot come up with a better alternative.

A factor further complicating the situation is the current, sharp disagreement concerning who ultimately should be in charge of defining what is ethical, defining what is acceptable, defining what is "right." This disagreement is not new to corporate America but has been escalating in recent years as employees have begun demanding more autonomy. It now seems to be coming to a head in light of Enron, Adelphia, Communications Martha Stewart, Tyco International, WorldCom, etc. and is the source of a great deal of confusion.

Traditional "bosses" continue to believe that they should do the defining in terms of what is right. These bosses view employees mainly as another set of machine parts to be manipulated in any way necessary to increase *efficiency* and to improve the bottom line. This philosophy is epitomized by "tough guys" such as Albert J. Dunlap, better known as "Chain Saw Al" who, according to the *New York Times* article, "Sunbeam Board, in Revolt, Ousts Job-Cutting Chairman," laid off about 20 percent of the workforce at Crown Zellerbach, one third of the workforce at Scott Paper, and more than 6,000 at Sunbeam before being fired.[1] Note that Dunlap was not fired because of his tactics but because he didn't produce the promised bottom-line results. In his book, *Mean Business,* Dunlap states, "If you see an annual report with the term 'stakeholder' in it, put the report down and run, don't walk away from the company... Companies such as these make major decisions that are more in tune with employees and the community than with stockholders... Employees are stakeholders, but they don't deserve rights the way shareholders do, unless they've invested some money in the company. We've gone way overboard in creating rights for everybody, and companies have been pulled into that mess... They keep thousands of people on their payrolls even when they clearly cannot afford such largesse and are putting the entire operation at risk... If you're in business, you're in business for one thing—to make money."[2]

These bosses are currently being confronted by a growing band of others who are thinking more in terms of *effectiveness* and who realize that the key to success is bringing the employees Mr. Dunlap feels such disdain for, to life. One side of the disagreement is held by the tough guys, such as Al Dunlap, who are locked into the "growth ethic" mentality and can think only in terms of *quantities* and *value-free* numbers (excluding the human values that shape the ethical climate of an organization). The other side is represented by managers moving toward the "development ethic" (which includes growth but also much more) who are beginning to think more in terms of *quality* and the importance of *value-full* employees to improved performance.

The confrontation is between the tough guys featured in a recent issue of a popular business journal who received recognition because they had the guts to wade into troubled company waters, take matters into their own hands, make the hard decisions, and cut hundreds or thousands of jobs; and the growing number of "not-so-tough" managers that Tom Peters talks about who instead see employees as the answer to the company's economic success, as a largely untapped reservoir of potential.

Finally, in the worst-case scenario, the confrontation is between the "me-I" egoists and the "we" leaders. The "me-I" managers see efforts to improve their organization's ethical climate, modernization efforts, quality improvement efforts, and reengineering efforts mainly as ways of demonstrating personal superiority. Such efforts provide ways to show the world that the managers are once again out ahead, on the cutting edge. The "we" managers are those who understand that in order to succeed such efforts require leaders who are willing to step back and to share the spotlight with their workforce.

It is relatively easy to tell these two groups apart. First the "me-I" bosses tend to be workaholics. They are driven to succeed, to win. They never stop competing. They have to beat everyone on the block. I do not know whether the cause is genetic or environmental but these people are unrelenting. The company is their lives; everything else is secondary. The worst part is that they expect and frequently demand that other employees demonstrate the same priorities. They look for lieutenants who have complete faith in their commander's judgment and who will leap to obey orders.

A second common characteristic is that "me-I" bosses overpay themselves. This group believes they deserve more dollars than anyone else because they make all the decisions. They believe they deserve continual salary increases despite the fact that the company (once you get past the hype and short-term number juggling) is not really doing too well. The "me-I" bosses firmly believe that they work harder, contribute more than anyone else, and therefore, earn what they are paid. The other side of the coin is that such outlandish salaries are one of the few success symbols "me-I" bosses enjoy. They cannot count on the workforce to applaud. They are not liked or respected by their employees. Feared, perhaps, but not respected.

As a result of this relationship, "me-I" bosses characteristically tend to spend as little time as possible with employees. When they *do* make business-hour appearances the purpose is to reaffirm the fact that they are in charge, not to win friends. The people they want to spend time with are other growth-oriented executives so they can compare salaries and numbers, so they can reinforce the belief that because their numbers are bigger than everyone else's, they have succeeded. Growth-oriented bosses also like to hang out with the Wall Street crowd. These people talk their language and are the key to realizing their wildest dreams in terms of compensation. If someone is called a "darling of Wall Street" you can be sure they're on the "me-I", growth-ethic side of the fence.

A fourth general characteristic of "me-I" bosses is that they like publicity and believe they deserve to be the organization's spokesperson. When an announcement is to be made, they make it. They are the ones who get interviewed. They are the ones who tour the country touting the success of their organization's change effort, even though it isn't really succeeding. Again, because they are not very popular in the workplace and because their personal lives have frequently atrophied, such recognition is critical to them. It helps them maintain the belief that they are successful.

One last characteristic is that "me-I" bosses are often consummate politicians. They spend a lot of time schmoozing. They are extremely good at networking. They belong to the right clubs. They sit on the right boards. They know whose support is needed to become more powerful and they know how to gain it. Everyone is a pawn in their game and they are the master, sliding about the board, manipulating, flattering, and bullying without any doubt or hesitation. They also tend to be paranoid. As a result, they are the most cunning and ruthless of street fighters.

Are "me-I" bosses considered unethical? Not by most accepted criteria. They might be disliked, but their behavior is not necessarily unethical. They are playing according to the rules introduced more than 100 years ago. At that point in history the concept of *laissez-faire* economics was introduced saying that *if we encourage every individual to pursue his or her own selfish interest, with as few restrictions and as little regulation as possible, society will benefit the most.* The workplace, therefore, should be viewed as an every-man-for-himself, dog-eat-dog arena where the strongest (the most ruthless?) feed off anyone they need to, jungle-style, in their rise to the top. In essence, you do what it takes to win.

BRINGING THE DARK SIDE TO LIFE

Now let us tie all this together into a fictional "me-I" boss so that we can gain a more focused perspective in terms of ethics. We will call our tough guy "Stanley." Stanley took over a Fortune 500 company several years ago that was in serious financial trouble due largely to increased foreign competition and the company's inability to adapt to a changing market environment.

The first thing Stanley did upon assuming command was to begin downsizing. He wanted to show rapid improvement in the bottom line by reducing salaries. Stanley, however, did not downsize all at once. Instead, he let it be known that everyone was expendable, then fired people whenever he felt the need. He said that his decisions were based on performance, although he was rarely present to see what employees were actually doing. When Stanley did make appearances it sent shock waves through the troops. He was known to throw people out of meetings when they disagreed with him. He was known to bawl out workers on the factory floor in front of peers, even to fire them on the spot to make a point.

When Stanley got an idea and wanted to discuss it, he did not hesitate to phone anyone he wanted as listeners, day or night, telling them where to meet him and how many minutes they had to get there. Intimidation was obviously a key ingredient of Stanley's management style. In part it was necessary because of the unreasonable situation he had put his employees in. He had cut staff mainly to improve the bottom line, not just to get rid of fat, so he had cut a lot of "muscle" away too. Employees able to quit and find new jobs on their own did so. The result was that the workload for those remaining increased tremendously. Stanley announced that the employees he favored would be those willing to work twelve hour days and seven-day weeks.

Stanley's need to succeed was compulsive. He was at the office constantly. He had little family life. If Stanley was willing to sacrifice his family life and perhaps his health for success he was certainly willing to sacrifice his workforce. The severance packages awarded to those laid off were one example of this willingness. At first the packages were reasonable, based on years of service and such. But then Stanley decided the company could not afford this expense and instead of laying employees off directly, he gave them a two-year, unpaid leave of absence. If they found another job during this period and were eventually called back, they lost their package. Most employees, of course, were forced to find another job. Most received calls shortly after doing so to come back, thus losing their package.

Despite, or more likely due to Stanley's efforts, the fortunes of the company continued to deteriorate. Eventually he and several Wall Street buddies decided that the best alternative was to buy it. Several years later, after the numbers at least had improved, this group of associates and shadow figures sold the company. Stanley made millions. And that is just the sad part of the story. The really sad part is that during this same period Stanley became a respected leader in the community. When Stanley was not at work, he was attending meetings. Stanley was a tireless go-toer. Or he would gather Rob and Stu and Jim together for a discussion over breakfast, gradually surrounded himself with a core of like-minded "me-I" guys, using these associates in tandem with well-placed but relatively small donations to help convince other community leaders of his eagerness and ability to guide their futures. His picture began to appear regularly in the local newspaper showing him introducing or discussing his latest project. Eventually he began lecturing wherever he could find an audience. One of his topics was the need to improve organizational ethics.

Despite the reality of his career, despite the obvious hypocrisy, despite the fact that most of the projects he took control of produced little besides more time in the spotlight for Stanley, a majority of the townspeople bought it. What we have here, once again, is the old story of the emperor's new clothes. People wanted to believe in Stanley because by laissez-faire standards, by the economic standards that businesses in the United States have been suckled on, he had succeeded. There were, of course, also plenty of less sophisticated gawkers in the crowd, current employees and ex-employees who saw that the regalness was merely a façade and sometimes said so. However, they said so in whispered voices hushed by fear of the retribution that would inevitably follow if they were heard.

So Stanley went happily on his way. He was now a "me-I" boss in his community as well and ran it basically the same way he had run his company, surrounding himself with loyal lieutenants who jumped to do his bidding, bullying or trying to discredit those who dared to oppose him. Eventually, however, the inevitable happened. People began to look beyond the talk and to realize that despite all the meetings, despite all the publicity, despite all the new efforts, very little of value was actually materializing. Stanley began to lose credibility. When he realized that fame and control were slipping away our hero took it with uncharacteristic, philosophical nonchalance. During an interview, when a reporter mentioned that people were beginning to suspect that his own agenda was more important to him than the community's Stanley simply shrugged his shoulders and said, "I'm about to retire. Why should I care?" Then he gathered up his millions and moved to Florida, perhaps to find a new challenge there.

LOOKING AT THE OTHER SIDE

Sound familiar? We all knows Stanleys, or milder versions of Stanley. Most of us do not like them, and do not want them for leaders. But they are going to be difficult to get rid of until we develop an appropriate standard by which to judge management's behavior. The "me-I" bosses have played by the rules and won. They have proven themselves the toughest of the tough. And they will not be denied.

So, once again, is their approach, or their attitude unethical? Stanley was a "winner" by currently popular standards. He did not break any laws, or at least none that can be proven. The public seemed to accept his behavior, even to honor it. However, there are still nagging doubts in the back of our minds. The way he won doesn't seem quite right for some reason.

Now let us move to the other end of the spectrum to talk about the not-so-tough guys who treat employees like human beings, who offer employees respect, who do not feel the need to dominate, and most amazingly, who allow their own success to be dependent on the character and expertise of their employees. In this instance we do not need to make up a fictional character. There are a growing number of live ones around who easily fill the bill. My count includes the top-level management of Motorola, W. L. Gore, Solectron, Harley Davidson, Semco, Men's Warehouse, Wegman's Food Market, Johnsonville Sausage, and L. L. Bean.

This list, fortunately, is getting longer each year. Perhaps the most prominent characteristics shared by these leaders are their inherent or learned respect for employees, their respect for employee potential, and their belief that management is responsible for facilitating the realization of that potential. Ralph Stayer, the CEO of Johnsonville Sausage, said that he believes it *immoral* for business leaders not to allow and encourage employees to develop their talents as fully as possible. And although what Stayer said may sound altruistic, it is not. Instead, in terms of effective management, it is good common sense.

The Hawthorne Study is the best-known of many such management studies proving beyond a doubt that people make more of an effort and accomplish more when they feel they are part of the team, when their opinion is sought and listened to. Employees try harder when management trusts them enough to couple authority with responsibility, when management identifies and addresses their needs in return for them working to meet the company's needs.

And, again, this attitude is not new. Not-so-tough-guys have been popping up and succeeding for some time now. In the late 1700s a man named Robert Owen became the manager of the largest textile mill in England. He made it the most profitable operation in the country by going against prevailing management wisdom, and treating his employees with respect. This was unheard of in those days, when workers were "owned" by businesses. Workers and their families lived in company housing and bought what they needed from the company store. In most instances the rent was excessive and the store prices so inflated that families were constantly in debt. During this period, owners believed that *as little as possible* should be invested in employees and *as much work as possible* should be forced out of them. Owen, instead, gave his employees shorter work hours, better-than-average dwellings (one room on two floors instead of one room on one floor), higher than average wages, education for all ages, and below-average prices at the store, reaping enormous financial rewards for his willingness to buck the system.

Did the other industrialists watch and learn something of value from Owen's innovative, more ethical approach? They watched. They most certainly watched, grinding their teeth all the while. But instead of learning from Owen's example, instead of incorporating Owen's ideas into their own operations they condemned him. They labeled him an eccentric and a threat to the stability of society. They said that his success was a fluke. They did everything possible to block the spread of reforms he proposed.

One has to wonder why.

In the early 1900s, Henry Ford again bucked conventional wisdom. He stunned the world when he doubled the standard wage while shortening the workday. Ford's belief was that if his employees earned enough to afford a car of their own, the entire economy as well as the Ford Motor Company would benefit. Ford, like Owen, also provided better housing, free education, inexpensive medical attention, and below-average prices at the company store for his employees. Though this strategy allowed him to become the most successful industrialist of his era, as well as the wealthiest man in the world, Henry Ford was, *once again*, condemned by his peers in the world of business as a dangerous radical and as a serious threat to society.

And, *once again*, we have to wonder why.

I must now ask, "Is the behavior of these not-so-tough-guys more ethical than that of the tough guys?" Instinctively, readers may want to say yes. But what is our standard? To make ethical judgments people need a standard by which to measure their response. Sometimes the standard is personal, but usually it is one that has been developed by society and tested by time. We need a standard that has been accepted universally or, at least, that is acceptable to the majority in order to make wise decisions.

Defining a standard by which to judge behavior is what ethics is about. Many such standards exist. People have been developing them for some time. But how do we define the most appropriate standard for our workplace situation? What do we base our choice on? Do irrefutable generic laws exist that delineate the difference between what is right and what is wrong? Does what is right and what is wrong vary according to each situation? Which is called upon first in terms of ethical decisions, the individual's belief system or the belief system supported by the company's culture?

Finally, perhaps the most important question in terms of our argument is, "How should a systemic perspective influence our attempts to identify the most appropriate ethical standard for the workplace?"

Obviously we have a lot of questions to find answers for.

Chapter 2

Tales From the Trenches

SETTING THE STAGE

Here's a story about two large bicycle-manufacturing companies that merged several years ago. Each company was very different. One was a rapidly growing importer and distributor of bicycles and bicycle parts. This company had an extremely entrepreneurial and aggressive culture with a hierarchical management structure. The reward system was rudimentary. The sales force worked for commissions that were very reasonable. The rest of the staff was on straight salary. The punishment system was equally simple; failure to meet one's required numbers led first to harassment, then demotion, then firing. However, the company was relatively successful and profitable, which made people want to stay (everybody likes to work for a winner), and although employees frequently put in sixty-hour weeks, there was little turnover.

The second company manufactured and imported bicycles. It was relatively new, had always belonged to a parent company, and rarely showed a profit. This company was run like a big family, with the father figure making all the decisions. Punishment took the form of counseling. All employees were salaried with a small bonus potential and increased their pay levels through regular raises.

It should have been obvious to those planning the merger that the management cultures of the two organizations had very little in common. However, the decision process never took management culture into consideration. Instead, somebody looked at the manufacturing and sales numbers and said, "Gee, if we get these two together we'll move to the head of the pack. We'll be one of the biggest." And bigger, of course, is better, or so the thinking goes.

Both companies believed that the expected growth in market share and the expected economies of scale would increase profitability. They also believed that because the future looked so bright employees from both firms would understand the need to do things differently. "But we don't have time to deal with the managerial issues now. We'll deal with them later. This is a wonderful opportunity and we don't want to miss it."

Wonderful opportunity or not, after losing $2 million during the first year the management team that arranged the merger left. A new CEO was hired, who worked to integrate operations that were redundant, or even in competition with each other. He also decided that an immediate reduction in overhead would improve the short-term bottom line, and make the company more attractive to investors. So he downsized. Layoffs began throughout the company, followed by cuts in brand names and distribution facilities. These cuts were followed by more layoffs.

The CEO and his small cadre of top-level managers made all their operational decisions based on the numbers, with no input from the employees who were affected. The cultural issues were still largely ignored. The CEO decided that there just wasn't enough time to consider cultural issues right now. Everyone was too busy improving productivity.

The downward spiral had begun. Within the next five years, the company lost another $30 million. People who could get out, got out. Another CEO was brought in. He also downsized to cut overhead and improve the financial numbers. The second new CEO then gave raises to the "survivors." However, each raise was coupled with an increase in job responsibilities. This was necessary to fill the void left by those who had been cut. The CEO also introduced a bonus system as an incentive for the sales force. Bonuses, however, were based on unrealistically high goals, making employees even more cynical and distrustful. Worker morale and commitment levels continued to decline. Field salespeople hired exclusively to sell the company's products took on additional lines from other firms. Managers hid expenses so as not to exceed budget. The level of internal theft increased. Employees seeking jobs elsewhere felt no qualms about releasing proprietary information in order to gain favor.

Does this story sound familiar? Are there ethical issues here? Yes, of course there are. First, employees at all levels were cheating the system—stealing, using company time to search for new jobs, falsifying records, and selling for other companies as well. Obviously the bicycle company should fire them and bring in new employees. But would bringing in new employees make a difference in the ethical climate? Would a new employee act any differently in the same cultural scenario? Probably not, because these actions are just symptoms of deeper problems embedded in the company's culture. In this case study, management had made the workforce situation hopeless. Employees had little or no ability to improve or to influence their work environment. They knew that the current CEO would not last much longer than his predecessors and that the next one would probably instigate another downsizing.

So who is to blame? It is obvious that top-level management did not do their homework thoroughly enough before the merger. They did not take the cultural issues or the people issues into account. So, whose fault is that? Did management ignore these factors on purpose? Was their goal to lose as much money as possible, while making life miserable for the employees? Management committed errors of judgment, yes, but not on purpose. It also suffered from those errors. Is making a mistake that unintentionally hurts others an unethical act? Most people would say no.

This leaves us with no culprit. The lower-level employees did unethical things in an effort to regain some degree of control over their lives and jobs. Upper-level managers created a climate that encouraged people to act unethically, because they did not fully understand the implications of the proposed merger. Could this situation have been avoided? It most certainly could have. If the two original companies, or even if the one merging company, had been managed in a systemic rather than a traditional manner, the problems identified in this scenario would have never come up, or they would have been dealt with immediately. In a systemically run organization, top-level management would have taken the issue of culture into account before carrying through the merger and with the appropriate assistance would have resolved it. The whole issue of who was acting ethically and who was not could have been avoided.

THE VIEW FROM ANOTHER ANGLE

Recently, I spoke to a young salesman from a small electronics firm. He told me this story about his organization's management culture.

"Our company is doing fairly well. We have sales of over $30 million and have shown a good profit during the last seven years. But the parent company keeps pushing us. At the end of each month panic erupts. The parent company keeps demanding increased sales. We have salespeople calling valued customers, begging them to accept shipments early so they can meet quotas. When this is done, of course, a shortage frequently occurs in the following month and the panic gets worse.

After a while I figured it out. The parent company sees us solely as a source of income, as a cash cow. I have never heard of anyone from headquarters visiting us. I know my bosses are embarrassed and upset by the way the parent company treats us, but they are afraid to say anything. They avoid questions from the rest of the workforce and keep everyone in the dark about what is happening.... No one has any idea of what the future holds. Everybody is uptight. Nobody trusts anyone. The managers keep to themselves. When anything happens, they immediately begin pointing fingers, trying to shift the blame instead of addressing the problem.

I'm beginning to understand that management in my company has been forced into a no-win situation. What they accomplish is never good enough. They get pounded on by the parent company. They, in turn, pound on us. They are just trying to survive until they can get out. Most of them have been with the company less than five years. Meanwhile, many of the line workers have been with the company twenty years or more and really care about it. But they can't do anything. They don't even dare make suggestions. The situation is killing morale.

In the purchasing department where I work it's dog eat dog. People do not share information or expertise.... Absolutely no mentoring is done. I had to start cold turkey. If I had known some of the things that I know now when I started, I could have saved the company a lot of money. And this lack of information is organization-wide. I have [no] idea of how what I do fits into the big picture. I once asked my boss if I could visit another department that I interact with a lot. He told me that if I didn't have enough to do with my time he would give me more work."

Does this story sound familiar? Is there anything unethical going on here? Once again, it depends on how we evaluate management styles. If we are speaking strictly from a traditional point of view, it is business as usual, or get the most possible productivity out of your employees for the least possible reward. Traditional management keeps employees at a distance so one doesn't have to worry about their needs as fellow human beings. Traditional management won't let employees see the big picture, but keeps them guessing.

However, if we decide to view employees as more than numbers on a tally sheet this approach runs into trouble. In the small electronics company scenario, the parent company viewed employees as resources to be squeezed continually for increased production, yet with no additional incentive. At the same time the employees were not asked to provide ideas for improving processes in order to help increase productivity. Employees were simply supposed to work harder, not smarter.

Aside from being primitive, is this approach to management unethical? Even more important from a systemic perspective, would a more humane approach in the workplace increase productivity? Again, ethics relates to setting standards for individual and group behavior. With this in mind, would it be right to set a standard regarding the treatment of employees? Should we define what is right and what is wrong when trying to improve the bottom line? Or would that be an infringement on an employer's rights?

How about setting reasonable production levels? How about rewarding employees for surpassing those same levels? Frederick Taylor, the father of Scientific Management, tried this back in the 1800s. Productivity increased immediately. But then the owners said that the workers had been holding back. The production level required to gain the bonus was raised. After that, every time employees surpassed the new level set it was raised again until, eventually, the workers quit trying, thus creating a losing situation for everyone involved.

Was it unethical that the employees stopped trying? Some people would say so. They would say that employees are paid to work as hard as they can, and that once the salary level is decided, employees who do not work hard are behaving unethically. Was it unethical that the owners kept raising the bar? Some people would say so. They would also say that from a pragmatic perspective, if increased profits were the objective, the owners were acting in an extremely short-sighted manner.

As you can see, there are many gray areas to consider when pondering ethical questions. How we address these gray areas depends upon what each individual thinks is important. It is obvious that no consensus exists. Behavior considered ethical by some might be considered unethical by others. Behavior considered ethical by owners and managers who are looking after their own interests is often considered unethical from a worker's point of view. Is it possible to find a standard that satisfies both groups, or is this the inherent dilemma of ethics?

TROUBLE IN THE NOT-FOR-PROFIT SECTOR AS WELL

Recently, I heard another story about a woman who was hired to develop and run a new services department for a hospital. Initially, she had been baffled by the lack of cooperation throughout the hospital. When she asked about it, her boss labeled it "resistance to change." Eventually, she realized that serious disagreement existed at the senior level of management over what the future of the organization should be and how the organization should be administered.

After months of discussion her department staff reached a consensus concerning what new services should be offered. However, this success was thwarted when managers from other departments began encouraging their staff directly or indirectly to impede or undermine the designing of these new services. For example, necessary information was frequently withheld. Members of my friend's staff talked about being victims of the famous "mushroom treatment" (being kept in the dark). They were frustrated because they frequently lacked the information necessary to do their jobs properly.

The new services manager explained, "In spite of what was going on, we did develop several new services and got them to the point where they were ready for the market. But before introducing them we had to generate required policies and procedures and have all hospital directors sign off on them. I was put in charge of facilitating the process of writing up the policies and procedures. My recommendation was to get input from every department affected. I asked that a multi-disciplinary task force of staff be formed and meet weekly. Task force members would take the meeting results back to their immediate managers for comment. Managers' comments would be presented at the next meeting. Once a month the managers themselves would get together to okay what had been completed.

With great excitement, I prepared for the first monthly meeting of managers. Task force members agreed that several policies were ready for approval. Everybody arrived on time for the meeting, but almost immediately the managers began excusing themselves to attend to other matters. By the end of the meeting, almost no one was left in the room, and not one policy had been approved. The same thing happened at the next monthly meeting. Eventually, I discovered that these people had axes to grind with each other and were more intent on seeing who could find the most fault with the others' recommendations, [and] on seeing who could best sabotage the others' ideas, than on getting something done.

At this point I decided to put the managers themselves in charge of designing the policies and procedures. My strategy worked, or, at least, I thought it worked. Because they were now directly responsible for producing results, the managers did eventually reach resolution on several issues. The next step, however, was to present these results to *their* bosses for *their* approval, and, to my chagrin, the questions and jockeying started all over again at that level.

As a result, up until now not one policy has been approved officially. But in practice this has become a moot point. Several of the services we initially proposed are already being offered. The policies and procedures designed by lower level staff are being followed by those directly involved despite the lack of approval from their superiors, who look the other way. It is a ridiculous situation. Even though I am a manager, it makes me wonder if management is really necessary in most instances."

Does this story sound familiar? There doesn't appear to be anything unethical happening, but management seems to have created a world of its own. Some members of management seem to be more interested in interdepartmental and inter-level intrigues than in defining and fulfilling the mission of the organization. In short, more competition seems to exist among the hospital's in-house units than between the hospital and its marketplace competitors. And the employees see themselves as pawns. They are unable to do their jobs correctly because of the lack of necessary input from other units. But, at the same time, they are held responsible for the results and are sacrificed when the situation calls for a scapegoat. They have been given responsibility, but then have been "disempowered" by management level organization politics.

Is management acting unethically? Probably not, but why are some managers blocking each other's efforts and, at the same time, limiting their employees' ability to do their jobs? Here is an example of a management culture that has lost its focus, or perhaps that never had a focus. Can such a situation be improved? Absolutely. It can be improved, but not until the culture has changed.

The next question must be, "How do organizations change such a culture?"

It's a lot easier than you might think, once people begin thinking systemically.

THE RIGHT IDEA DOESN'T GUARANTEE SUCCESS

The next organization discussed operated more on the positive end of the culturally progressive management scale. It was a division of one of our country's largest insurance companies and was organized to serve one specific customer group that includes millions of potential customers. Until several years ago, the division's contract was guaranteed by the government.

Approximately four thousand people were employed by this organization. Eventually, the CEO decided the training program for employees was inadequate. Training was sporadic and was dictated either by top-level management, or by the training department. The CEO decided that a more effective approach was required, and that employees might be a good source of information for the design of this approach.

A group of employees, representing all functions and levels, gathered to begin the design effort. First, the design team decided that a corporate-wide training network should be formed and should be served by a centralized database. Process criteria were developed, including:

- All employees should have the chance to help define training needs
- All employees should have access to the full range of training and education opportunities available.

An Education Council including representatives from every department and every level was created to oversee and integrate the effort. The Education Council helped shape voluntary groups and gave them time off from work to identify problems and to discuss potential solutions. One of the problems identified was the employee evaluation system. Employees were allowed to redesign the system developing a two-way approach with managers evaluating employees and employees evaluating managers.

This insurance company was in the early stages of a successful move toward systems thinking and systemic management. Results were already obvious in terms of productivity, employee morale, and customer satisfaction. The company still had a long way to go, but executives and managers were starting to understand the value of the cultural change they were experiencing.

Then something happened. Those representing the customer population decided that a better price might be found if the contract was put out for bid. There is nothing wrong with that; it's called "free enterprise." The troublesome part, at least for this company and for its early-phase systemic thinking was the result if this decision focused only on the numbers.

Another firm might come along willing to risk all in order to win the contract. Its management would have to understand the experience-based advantages enjoyed by the current holder of the contract. Its management would also have to understand that there was little chance of outdoing the current holder in terms of service quality. That would leave only price as a competitive lever, and in order to provide the lowest bid, the competitor would obviously have to cut overhead.

From past examples we know what this means. The now-familiar rationale would sound something like this. "If we lay off ten percent of our workforce, we'll probably be able to win the bid. The current holder will have trouble following suit because they are working to become more participative and, as a result, have been forced to make job security a priority. With us the layoff will mean that everyone we keep will have to work longer and harder for the same wages. But at least the remaining employees will still have their jobs. That should provide some solace. We'll deal with the morale issue later. Once we get the contract we can make it up to them."

And here we go again.

If this scenario were to come true, it would most likely result in a lose-lose-lose situation. In order to beat the competitor's bid, the original firm would have to begin cutting costs immediately. In order to do so effectively on such short notice it would have to lay off employees as well. This, of course, would spell the demise of the new systemic culture as well as all trust toward top-level management. Since trust is the most important ingredient of any successful organization improvement effort, the original company's service to customers would deteriorate.

If the competitor won the contract, it would have at least two immediate problems. Employees would have to deal with the difficulties inherent in learning the special needs of a new client. At the same time, management would have to struggle with the systemic and morale problems that inevitably result from a downsizing. There is little chance that the new company would be able to meet the service expectations of the customer.

In the long run, therefore, (and perhaps even in the not-so-long-run) everyone would lose as a result of the customer representative's focus on price alone. Let us hope that the representative was a little more far-sighted.

Can any of the potential actions in this example be considered unethical? I do not think so. But still, what might happen (because of a focus on price) does not *seem* right. For some reason the contract-holding company has realized that the development of employee potential is critical to long-term success and has begun taking steps necessary to insure that development. Then, another "hungry" company comes along that is willing to do whatever it must to take the contract away. The first company understands the importance of job security to the development of employee potential. The second company sees the willingness to downsize as its only way to compete.

At least one company (but most likely both companies) will end up cutting staff to give customers a cheaper price. As a result, the customer will almost definitely receive a product of lesser quality, no matter who "wins." Does this make sense in terms of the big picture? The question is, "How do we protect the efforts to develop employee potential necessary to increased long-term productivity and quality in a culture fixated on improving the short-term bottom line through short-term measures?"

Does this sound familiar? Even if nothing unethical is going on here, something is obviously out of whack. What we find portrayed in this scenario is illogical behavior, at least in terms of individual and societal development.

THIS TIME, FROM THE INDIVIDUAL PERSPECTIVE

Marcia had just taken a job as a loan officer for a sub-prime mortgage refinancing lender. In terms of compensation she had agreed to a base salary plus commission. Her goal, set by management, was $250,000 a month in loans. She was told that if her intake fell below the $250,000 mark for two consecutive months she would lose her job. Marcia was a single parent raising three children. She was energetic. She needed to earn money and had no problem putting in extra hours. Marcia felt that she would do well with this job. She had been in sales most of her life and was very customer-oriented.

During April, her first month, Marcia brought in $265,000 worth of business. During May, she brought in only $210,000 worth. In June, however, she sold to several big customers and brought in $1,500,000 worth. In July, she brought in only $165,000. At that point her boss warned her that if she didn't hit the $250,000 mark again in August, she would be terminated. Marcia was flabbergasted. She asked if the $1,500,000 could be carried over? It would fill her quota for half a year. Her boss said, "No." Each month was a new beginning, allowing their lenders to carry excesses from good months over to the next would not be in the best interest of the company.

One of Marcia's coworkers took her aside and told her she had made a mistake in finishing all the deals she had set up in June. Marcia had received a large commission for that month, but at the possible cost of her job. The coworker said Marcia had to learn to "sandbag," to spread out her good months, to start each month with something in reserve. Marcia asked if "sandbagging" was ethical? The coworker shrugged and said, "That's not the point. The point is, do you want to keep your job or not? You have no choice."

So Marcia began "sandbagging," sometimes stringing out her negotiations with customers, sometimes "adjusting" the month-end figures she submitted to her employer. Was she acting unethically?

You decide.

Once again, from the systems perspective, Marcia's problem had more to do with the culture she worked in and with the way the reward process was set up than with herself. *We do not change an organization's culture by focusing on individuals, by changing the habits of individuals, or by working on the attitudes of individual employees. We change an organization's culture by first looking at the systems shaping that culture, then by redesigning those systems so that they produce the desired results.*

Behavior is shaped mainly by cultural systems. In the workplace, the behavior of employees is shaped mainly by the management culture, i.e., by the management systems in place.

Ethical behavior and management systems, the two are inseparable. The purpose of this book, therefore, is to help us discover a design for management systems that will encourage positive employee behavior.

But first, we need to revisit the question of what, exactly, constitutes ethical behavior.

Making Sense Out Of Ethics

SO WHAT IS GOING ON?

Not one of the five scenarios presented in Chapter 2 is unique. The situations described are occurring in organizations throughout the country and are limiting their effectiveness and hurting their productivity.

In the bicycle company study, the precipitating problem was a blind pursuit of growth. The prospect of becoming larger than any competitor was too much of a temptation for those in control. The potential risks of the involved merger were either minimized or ignored.

In the electronics firm scenario, the main problem could be defined as one of greed, or perhaps more diplomatically, as one of a lack of perspective. Parent company management wanted the most profit for the least expenditure. Those at the top viewed only quantifiable factors of the operation as important to the quest for improved profits, completely ignoring non-quantifiable factors such as employee morale, employee experience, and employee ideas.

In the hospital case study the main problem was one of in-house competition. Managers of the various departments saw each other as a threat. The work of the various units was poorly integrated. Each department functioned like a feudal kingdom, with managers jealously guarding their kingdom's borders, throwing stones at anything that moved on the other side of the wall.

In the insurance company scenario, the main problem was the customer representative's inability (the original company did eventually lose the contract) to take quality of service into account when choosing a provider. Short-term price was the sole determinant of the winning bid. The idea that the original company had changed its culture and now focused on improving the quality of service offered rather than on immediate customer saving was not a consideration.

In scenario number five the problem was the loan company employee evaluation system. The monthly "goal" of $250,000 was established to insure loan officer productivity. In reality, this approach quickly burned people out.

Having to reach the established goal every month with no carryover possible generated a great deal of stress. In addition, the involved requirement forced employees to act unethically just to keep their jobs. This company chose to use fear as the driving force in its management system. As a result, the level of turnover in the company was very high. High turnover, of course, hurt the company and negatively affected profits.

So what *is* going on? All five scenarios show situations that could, or did, lead to bottom-line losses and to a miserable work environment. In each study the managers involved must have known what was happening. So why did they allow the situations to occur? Why did they allow the problems to continue?

These five sketches together illustrate the central issue addressed in this book. Each scenario is different, but all are driven by the same cultural force; all five are driven by the same problem. The problem is that most individuals and companies in the United States are still hooked on *winning*, which in this sense means *beating* somebody else. Most for-profit and frequently non-profit organizations are hooked on being bigger, on having their numbers grow faster than anyone else. Notice the excitement, the publicity, the swell of pride every time the Dow Jones Industrial Average hits a new high. At the same time, notice how little attention is paid to those who suggest that the underpinnings of these numbers might be rotting away. The list of modern-day companies suspected of falsely representing corporate strength is long, including Lucent Technologies, Enron, Adelphia Communications, Arthur Anderson, ImClone, Tyco International, and WorldCom. And these, according to some experts, represent just the tip of the iceberg.

There is nothing wrong with winning, nor is there anything wrong with growth in itself. The desire to achieve both is healthy. But when an individual or a company or a society becomes obsessed with winning, with growing, and when no sacrifice becomes too great in order to do so, then the overall cost in terms of individual, corporate, and societal development eventually begins to outweigh the benefit.

The United States has generated the wealthiest and most powerful economy in the world. The corporate leaders driving this economy want to stay on top. They are proud of their success and are loathe to permit anything, even reality, to disturb their celebration. Yet at the same time, our corporate leaders are not stupid. They know that more productive ways of managing organizations are being developed. They know that research has proven in-house competition detrimental to productivity, and that a focus on the numbers alone can be counterproductive. They know that they must continue to learn and to adapt if they wish to maintain their economic lead.

In order to learn what is necessary, industrial leaders in the United States have visited companies that do things differently, both at home and abroad. These companies have gotten rid of in-house competition, and have begun taking into consideration factors that are not quantifiable. Industrial leaders have studied these companies, viewed the results in person, and have returned from their visits brimming with new, exciting ideas they want to incorporate into their own organizational culture.

The faltering begins when these leaders realize how long the desired changes are going to take, and how much resistance there will be to the transition. A lot of employees will be threatened by what is proposed. These people will fight it. Also, the leaders must deal with the realization that the desired cultural changes can't be implemented piecemeal. Absolutely every employee who will be affected has to be involved, and that takes more time.

One major obstacle to cultural change in corporations is that we don't seem to have the "more time" necessary to implement the process correctly. The Japanese, following World War II, started basically with nothing, with a "greenfield" economic situation. When you start with nothing, making changes in what you design is relatively easy. The Japanese could reshape their management culture almost at will until things fit correctly. Other companies in the Asian economic block have more recently become serious competitors in the world market, taking advantage of this same flexibility of newness.

On the other hand, the United States is currently saddled with the largest and most complex industrial establishment in economic history. This situation decreases flexibility. For every new idea discussed or implemented, something old and highly successful by traditional standards must first be questioned and then dismantled. While it took the Japanese some thirty years to build their corporate culture virtually from scratch, while it is taking other new Asian economic powers even less time, it is probably going to take organizations in the United States much longer to accept the changes in management culture critical to on-going economic success.

Once again *time* is the culprit. New competitors are not about to cut us any slack. Every time corporate America pauses to think something through, the competitors gain market share. To make matters even worse, the private sector is not receiving adequate support and encouragement from the country's economic institutions. Company owners, stockholders, and especially the financial institutions that control corporate investment are impatient. They are not about to tolerate any downswing in productivity or any drop in short-term profits considered unnecessary, no matter how obvious the long-term benefits might be.

Most individuals and firms involved in financing our economy work on a commission basis. When the bottom line of the companies represented improves, their situation improves. They are totally focused, therefore, on the immediate numbers, on making these numbers look good so that the stock will sell, so that the customers' desire to invest will increase. What has to be done to make these numbers improve is of little concern.

As a result, some believe that from the most flexible of business cultures, the United States has evolved into one of the most rigid. Companies are forced by financial considerations to stick with the old methods and to continue managing by the numbers. Management teams are being forced to squeeze a little more, and then a little more profit out of the workforce using antiquated practices.

So what can be done? Traditionally, when faced with a problem the first step is to dissect it and to identify the cause. *I, of course, believe that the major producer of organizational, and of societal inability to change is the lack of an appropriate standard upon which to base decisions that include an ethical component.* It is the hesitation felt when faced with such decisions that thwarts change. This hesitation might come from an unwillingness to acknowledge the fact that an ethical component is, indeed, part of almost every choice. While the individuals involved might refuse to acknowledge this fact, they know intuitively that it is true, that the ethical component is there, and that it must be dealt with if the desired change is to succeed.

However, before the ethical component in any situation can be dealt with effectively it must be understood. An identified standard must exist against which it can be measured. This standard, in turn, must be rooted in the social philosophy of the culture involved. *The problem is that the business sector of the United States, though it most certainly can be seen as possessing cultural characteristics, has, thus far, not put much effort into developing a social philosophy from which such a standard can be gleaned.*

The United States was born during the same historical period as the *laissez-faire* theory of economic growth. Our economy was weaned on it and flourished because the *laissez-faire* approach works best when resources are unlimited, and the young United States offered that kind of opportunity. Alexis de Tocqueville, a French social historian who traveled through the country in 1831, said that immigrants arrived filled with excitement over solid mountains of salt and iron, of lead, copper, silver and gold, over cornfields waving and rustling in the sun, over "limitless riches, unimaginable stores of wealth and power.... To their minds, every new method that led by a shorter road to wealth, every machine that spared labor, diminished the cost of production ... seemed the grandest effort of the human intellect ... [this mindset], however, spawning a sordid and practical materialism which asked nothing of ideas, of the arts, and of science but their application toward ends of use and profit."[1]

Vernon Parrington, a great literary historian and teacher who wrote during the early 1900s, added that freedom (in the early United States) was interpreted to mean "the natural right of every citizen to satisfy his acquisitive instinct by exploiting the national resources in the measure of his shrewdness."[2] And, finally, one of the country's most respected historical figures, Benjamin Franklin, summed this attitude up quite simply by reminding us that, "Time is money."

The problem is that while the United States is driven by a theory of economic growth (laissez-faire) that seems to have worked quite well, it has never generated an appropriate theory of societal development for the economic growth to support. We have deluded ourselves into believing that our so successful economic philosophy can serve both purposes.

This arrangement does not work. A society's economic philosophy *must* support and be subservient to its social philosophy, as well as to the ethical standard that is drawn from its social philosophy. The economic philosophy cannot be allowed to dominate. It is too focused. It does not pay proper attention to a wide range of non-economic factors that are also critical.

In order to continue progressing, therefore, the United States must take the time to define its philosophy of social development. But before doing so, it must understand the foundational pieces. It must backtrack through the world of ethics to the study of philosophy that began in the western world with the Greeks, approximately three thousand years before the birth of Christ. This is where both ethics and the standard we seek find their roots.

PHILOSOPHY, STILL SOMETHING WE NEED

Academicians, religious philosophers, business leaders, and politicians have been arguing ethical issues for centuries now. They have divided into camps and have battled each other with words and, in some cases, with actions. Each camp has developed its own logic, and its own evidence. Each camp has been sure that it is right, although its foundational beliefs might differ radically from those of the opposition.

All of this has led to confusion in the workplace. However, the effect of this confusion has not been as great as one might expect. While ethics has been a buzzword of long standing, while employees are shunted periodically to seminars where they discuss case studies and role-play, while ethics is a required subject and must be incorporated into the course work of MBA programs, ethics training in actuality remains an embellishment to, rather than a core ingredient of most operations.

This statement should not cause alarm. Training in ethics might not be necessary in most operations. A majority of employees already want to do the "right" thing and are pretty good at figuring out what that is. This tendency comes, in part, from early religious conditioning, be it Buddhism, Christianity, Judaism, Hinduism, or Islam. The core teachings of all traditional religions encourage followers to "do the right thing." At the same time, the fact cannot be ignored that some of the most religious societies in our world exhibit the most corrupt business practices while some of the least religious societies exhibit the most ethical. So religion, at least in its present form, might not be as effective a deterrent as we wish to believe.

The desire to do the right thing is also instilled by nonreligious elements of society, by our education system, our legal system, and by everyday social interaction. Finally, this desire might even be passed along genetically. It might be intuitive. We might be born with it.

As a society develops its positive potential, as the level of available wealth grows, as education and skill levels rise, as overall health improves, less need seems to exist for an outside force to keep people on track, to help them deal with their frustrations, with the inexplicable, with the uncontrollable. People are gaining the tools necessary to help explain the inexplicable themselves. They are gaining an increasing amount of control over their lives.

Does societal progress decrease the need for an ethical belief system? I think not. Rather, as a society progresses, less need exists for religious and other educational institutions *to take control of* members' lives, *to teach* them the right thing, *to condition* them to think ethically using the fear of consequences as encouragement. At the same time, an ethical model or models are still needed for people to learn from and compare, perhaps picking one model for their own, perhaps combining pieces from several to create a new model.

One of the things we are now talking about is the difference between *teaching* and *learning*. We all have been taught. The teacher provides information he has decided we need to know concerning a specific subject. We are expected to absorb that information. Then we are tested in some way to make sure that we understand it. But how many of us have been given the opportunity to learn? How many of us have been put into a situation where relevant information is made available, but we are required to build our own models and to define our own answers? The number of those who have enjoyed such an experience, fortunately, is growing.

The swing in advanced societies is naturally toward *learning* and away from *teaching*. But even in a learning situation we need access to alternatives to draw from. The most perplexing issue in our search for foundational blocks upon which to build an individual ethical model is that so many alternatives exist and that the main ones usually contradict each other.

The challenge, therefore, is how to pick from radically opposed schools of thought, all of which have strengths. Or, perhaps more useful, the challenge is discovering how to combine these schools in a way that carries us to a higher level, that incorporates the strengths of each and eliminates the weaknesses.

This challenge is found not only in the world of ethics, but also in the realm of philosophy, which, as we have said previously, is the wellspring of ethical thought, the soil from which all ethical arguments gain their sustenance. It is in the realm of philosophy, therefore, that we must begin our quest.

Philosophy evolved as the result of man's attempt to understand the nature of reality. The two most foundational and traditional philosophical schools are *rationalism* and *empiricism*. The early rationalists believed that *ultimate truths* existed, and could be discovered intuitively once we were able to see through all the debris in our minds. Rationalists spent centuries searching for such truths, for even one such truth that could not be questioned. They believed that a preordained order existed in the universe and that once we found a way to tap into it all would become clear.

The empirical school of philosophical thought emerged in the fifteenth century, due to the realization that even if the rationalists could, indeed, define an ultimate truth or, perhaps, a system of ultimate truths, the value of these truths would be limited in terms of improving the overall quality of life. *Scientific method*, however, a fairly new kid on the block at that point in history (though one with ancient roots), demonstrated the ability to generate continuous improvement, at least in terms of the material world. Scientific method was not interested in discovering ultimate truths. Rather, *it was interested in discovering useable truths through testing and observation*. If the same combination of natural forces or human actions or ingredients produced the same results every time under the same circumstances it could be assumed that this combination would continue to do so in the future. Empiricism was built around the search for such useable truths.

During this period, the Church supported rationalism and led the search for ultimate truths. The battle between it and the new empiricists was fierce. The battle began in earnest during the Renaissance. Emphasis during this period, roughly 1250–1400, was increasingly on the individual. People were beginning to think for themselves rather than depending on the Church for answers, and empiricism supported their growing desire for independence.

By the time western society reached the Enlightenment Period (1500–1750) useable truths at least were no longer regarded as beyond the ordinary man's grasp. Galileo (1564–1612) said, "Pretending that the truth is so deeply hidden from us that it is hard to distinguish it from falsehood is quite preposterous; the truth remains hidden only while we have nothing but false opinions and doubtful speculations; but hardly has the truth made its appearance than its light will dispel dark shadows."

The Church, as one might suspect, found his efforts threatening and unwelcome. Galileo was eventually summoned to appear before the Inquisition on charges of heresy and spent the last part of his life under arrest. But the trend in the evolution of philosophy toward endowing every individual with the power to learn and to define at least useable truths could not be stopped.

AN EVENTUAL COMING TOGETHER

Rene Descartes (1596–1650) continued development of the rationalistic approach. He said that we must discern between the mind that defines reality, and our senses that create distractions from our quest. He said that we must seek the "truths" upon which reality is based through the intellect, and that our intellect contains innate ideas, not the product of experience, which allow us to discern what is true. He said that by using our intellect to ferret out what is true we can shape our own fate, rather than leaving it up to a divine authority.

John Locke (1632–1704) represented the empirical school during this period. He did not believe that we were born with the innate ability to differentiate truths. Rather, he said that the mind begins as "a blank sheet of paper" upon which experiences are recorded. From these experiences we build our own filter and use that filter to discover important truths.

David Hume (1711–1776) carried empiricism to its logical extreme. He said that our ideas arise solely from the impressions gained through our experiences, and that the same object, the same experience does not necessarily leave different individuals with the same impression. He said that no natural law guarantees a cause and effect relationship between events and their results, or between objects and the impressions they leave. He said that cause and effect is determined solely by experience. If the same stimulus is followed by the same response enough times people can safely *assume* that it causes that response. Following this logic Hume said that values are shaped solely by human nature and experience rather than by a higher authority. What we decide to believe is totally up to us.

During this period, efforts also began to wed the two foundational schools of philosophical thought—rationalism and empiricism. It was (and still is) understood, or at least widely believed that people need a set of beliefs, a *standard* (sound familiar?) upon which to build their individual reality, and their society. It was (and still is) understood at the same time that scientific method, or the actualization of empiricism, can greatly benefit us in terms of improving our quality of life.

The efforts of Emmanuel Kant (1724–1804) to integrate these two schools are perhaps the best known. The essence of Kant's argument was that laws or "truths" do, indeed, exist, but that man himself creates them based on a combination of analytical and synthetic knowledge. Kant argued that not one, but two types of knowledge exist. The first, called "analytical," is *a priori* and results from judgments in which the truth is validated by comprehension of the terms used, this comprehension being largely intuitive. Kant said that the second type of understanding, "synthetic," is *a posteriori* and results from judgments that require testing and proving, thus bringing science into the picture.

Kant's solution to the greatest philosophical challenge of the day, however, was not accepted by all (at least partially because it was so difficult to understand) and new, more sophisticated schools feeding off the original rationalism and empiricism appeared.

In relatively modern times the pragmatists, including Charles Pierce, William James, and especially John Dewey (1845–1952), once again attempted to wed the two warring factions. They said that ultimate truths do, indeed, exist. But instead of spending time trying to discover them so that people can work *from* them we should concentrate on working *toward* them. These philosophers said that the process of working toward such truths was the valuable part of the exercise. They also said that the most effective pattern of inquiry for our quest would be determined by what worked best, by what produced the best results. This, of course, opened the door to experience and science, allowing them to become our guide.

One more pragmatist whose work should be mentioned is E. A. Singer. While teaching at the University of Pennsylvania during the middle of the 20th century Singer made a contribution important to this discussion. Singer defined more clearly the link between pragmatism and rationalism. His predecessors had accepted the rationalists' quest for ultimate truths despite its apparent hopelessness. The early pragmatists had said, "Whether or not such truths are discoverable, or even exist for that matter is not really important for, you see, it is the *quest* that counts, it is the quest that we benefit most from."

Singer, however, announced that ultimate truths *do*, in fact, exist, lots of them. Singer said that they exist in the form of *ideals*. Now an "ideal" according to the dictionary is a conception of something in its absolute perfection that exists only in the mind. So *ideals*, by definition, are unachievable. But at least now people could give their ultimate truths a shape; at least now people could give them an essence rather than groping around in the dark for they knew not what. Also, perhaps just as important, with Singer's approach in hand *each individual could now define his or her own ideals; each society could now define its own ideals.*

The down-side of this scenario, of course, is that society currently lacks a *meta-ideal*, or (here it comes again) a standard against which to measure individual ideals, a standard that gives people some feel for the appropriateness of their ideals.

Before addressing this issue, however, it is necessary to add another piece to the puzzle. Now that the foundational philosophical building blocks are in place we need to progress on to the realm of ethics. We need to introduce the various existing schools of thought concerning how best to decide what is *right*, and to compare their strengths and weaknesses.

Chapter 4

Is It "Me-I" or "We"?

UTILITARIANISM REIGNS

Due at least in part to the symbiotic relationship existing between the realms of philosophy and ethics, the latter can also be defined in terms of conflicting theories. But in the case of ethics we are able to identify *two* sets of major rivals (utilitarianism versus egoism and deontology versus relativism) rather than just one (rationalism versus empiricism).

The first pair of opposed schools of thought includes *utilitarianism* and *egoism*. Utilitarianism says that the best answer to an ethical problem is that which provides the greatest good for the greatest number. Parallels can obviously be drawn between the utilitarian school of ethical thought and the pragmatic school of philosophical thought. Egoism, at the other end of the spectrum, says that people should focus solely on satisfying their own self-defined self-interest. This mindset is familiar too and can also, interestingly enough, be related to pragmatism, but it relates to what I shall call "the dark side" interpretation of pragmatism.

In western society both of these schools of ethical thought have been around since the beginning. In Europe, however, during the period following the decline of the Roman Empire and the loss of the economic stability that the Empire had previously provided (road systems, trading centers, laws, etc.), utilitarianism prevailed. This dominance occurred for two reasons.

First, Europe had sunk into what is now called the Dark Ages. It had fragmented into a hodge-podge of kingdoms, each nobleman staking out his own territory, building his fortress (usually on a hill in the middle of the territory), gathering into his community field hands and craftsmen to provide food and wares in return for his protection. This system of governance was called *feudalism* and led to almost constant warfare as the various domains battled it out, usually over land or other resources necessary to survival.

The second reason was the Catholic Church, the only thing binding this checkerboard of dukedoms and princedoms and kingdoms together. Because it reached into every domain the Church had an overview of how the pieces fit together. It was the only force that could talk to everyone, or that could get the different lords to talk to each other. It was the only force that could mediate and manipulate. The Church in those days was the closest thing the European continent had to a central government.

Most people were locked into a struggle for survival during the Dark Ages and the ensuing Medieval Period. If you lived through childbirth and infancy (a two-in-five chance) you were lucky if you reached your thirties. By your middle and late twenties you were entering old age. A major cause of such rapid physical deterioration was the almost universal poverty that existed. Famines occurred regularly due to droughts, wars, and intrigues. Epidemics of bubonic plague decimated the population.

At the same time, Europe was isolated from the rest of the world. Individual noblemen and their kingdoms were generally isolated from each other. Individual villages were isolated, and could not easily get help during periods of shortage. Usually, you were born into a village, grew up, married, and died there, without straying far afield. The only real reason for travel was to fight battles against the armies of neighboring lords.

Individual population centers were largely self-dependent. Little trade between them occurred even during periods of peace and plenty. At the same time, technology was still in a primitive state, having not progressed much over the last several hundred years. Farm work was done mostly by hand. Craftsmen worked with rudimentary tools they fashioned themselves and generated the power required for production through their own exertion.

As a result of this situation very little wealth was accumulated. Most money went to the Church or to the nobility, in the form of taxes. The remainder had to provide for the entire community. In such a close-knit society, most people were related in some way so that selfishness was hard to get away with. At the same time, the Church developed the concept of "one just price." Craftspeople were allowed to charge only enough to make a reasonable living. Charging more was considered a sin.

Under the guidance of the Church, guilds were formed to help regulate commerce in individual communities and, eventually, in cities. A *guild* included all the craftsmen who sold one product, be it shoes or houses or wheelbarrows. The guilds' three main responsibilities were to limit the number of craftsmen manufacturing that product, to decide how many items each member of the guild should be allowed to produce, and to set a price that was acceptable to the Church. Their objective was to make sure no members of the guild starved because they couldn't sell their wares due to a saturated market or because competitors were out-producing or under-pricing them.

The greatest good for the greatest number, the utilitarian approach was very much so in evidence during the Medieval Period when we talk in terms of the workplace, when we talk in terms of the economy. While the political world of that era was driven by egoism, (every lord for himself) the common people—the farmers, the townspeople, the tradesmen—in order to survive, were locked into utilitarianism. They were forced to cooperate whether they wanted to or not.

This emphasis lasted until crusades to recapture the Holy Lands triggered the Renaissance. Pope Urban II decided, for a variety of reasons (mostly nonreligious), that it was time to free these lands from the domination of the Islamic Empire. Over a period of several years he sent armies from a number of European countries to do so. While these armies failed miserably in terms of achieving military objectives, their travels, and the contacts they made with foreign cultures, as well as the maps they collected broke the European continent's isolation.

Trading partners were developed in the Middle East and then in the Far East. Ships sailed across oceans to discover new and more advanced cultures, as well as new sources of raw materials and finished goods. The merchant class, enfeebled since the decline of the Roman Empire, was reborn, with men rising rapidly to power and generating wealth by buying in one place and selling in another. As a result of such economic revitalization, the ability of the guilds and, ultimately, of the Church to regulate the distribution of existing wealth dissipated rapidly, overwhelmed by the steadily growing stream of profit pouring in.

EGOISM REARS ITS HEAD

The workplace ethic during the Renaissance switched from utilitarianism to egoism. This transition began in Italy, through whose ports (especially Venice) goods from Arab, Indian, and Oriental cultures flowed. This new egoism took the form of what has been called *Machiavellian Humanism*. The Italian merchants revived the ancient Greek humanistic belief that the purpose of life was not to prepare for the next world, but to develop and enjoy our positive human potential to the fullest possible extent *in this life*. At the same time, however, the merchants added their own unique twist. They said that in order to do so, in order to develop and enjoy one's potential, it was acceptable to take advantage of others. Several of the most successful trading families, the Medici family being one and the Borgias family being another, were famous for their adherence to this belief, leaving behind a trail of bodies during their economic ascendancy.

Another thing driving egoism during this period was the "scarcity mentality." Money has traditionally been a scarce, but extremely critical resource. During the Medieval Period, the wealth that did exist, as we have said, was controlled mainly by the Church and by the nobility, the two chief employers of the time. The peasant class, which made up more than ninety percent of the population, had access to almost none. These people grew or collected foodstuffs from the forest and made by hand the wares necessary to their survival. The other class, the craftsmen, was relatively small. Because they were controlled by guilds and by the Church-driven concept of one just price, most craftsmen could expect, once again, to sell their products for just enough to afford some of the most basic comforts.

All this changed with the advent of the Renaissance. Excess wealth was generated through trade, through advances in technology, and through the improvement of Europe's political and physical infrastructure. People realized quickly that excess wealth was the key to an improved quality of life. But not nearly enough wealth was being generated for everybody to benefit. Competition and conflict erupted over this critical resource. Thus arose the *scarcity mentality*. People with wealth hoarded it, were unwilling to share, and always wanted more as insurance against loss. People who lacked wealth were frequently willing to do whatever necessary to take it away from those who possessed it.

As the amount of wealth generated first by European and then by the western world's economic endeavors continued to increase, one would think that competition would subside. This was not the case, however. In truth, the competition grew steadily fiercer, and did not subside until governments intervened, introducing the concept of *economic socialism* and making it non-beneficial to continue accumulating wealth after a certain level was reached. In strongly socialistic societies the government also began insuring that all citizens had access to the resources necessary for the development of individual potential—food, shelter, medical attention, education, and employment. As a result the scarcity mentality faded until, in some instances, it has largely disappeared.

The United States, conversely, while the government has intervened to a limited degree, remains strongly *laissez-faire*. Thus, in the United States the scarcity mentality continues to dominate. Increasing individual wealth remains the primary objective for most. As a result of this trend the United States suffers the greatest gap between the wealthy and the poor in the developed world.

On one hand we have a growing number of millionaires and even billionaires who feel no qualms about using their wealth to influence government decisions in ways that protect and even allow them to increase this wealth. At the same time, a large percentage of this same wealthy segment of the population continues to argue that we should cut developmental government services for the less fortunate including education, health care, and job training, etc. They say that these services cost too much, push taxes too high, and slow economic progress when such progress is key to our nation's advancement.

This mind-set is called "trickle-down economics." It is nothing new, and at least partially because of the scarcity mentality, it has never worked. Trickle-down economics says let the wealthy keep what they earn, don't make them give any of it back to the government for redistribution, and, eventually, the wealthy will use their money in ways that benefit society.

Historically, this has never happened. Rather, the gap between the wealth and the rest of society has continued to grow until governments were forced to step in and to introduce constraints in the form of laws and taxes.

MORE PROBLEMS WITH UTILITARIANISM AND EGOISM

At this point we will focus on the utilitarian belief that the most ethical decision is that which generates the greatest good for the greatest number. One question that arises must be, "How do we define the greatest good?" Are we talking, for example, about the short term or the long term? A company lays 10,000 employees off, claiming that the move is necessary to the financial health of the organization, that the investors, i.e., the most critical stakeholder group, are demanding an improved bottom line. Obviously there are more investors than laid-off employees. Therefore, is the layoff the most ethical decision?

Judging by what has been going on largely unchallenged in the United States world of business, it would seem so. It is interesting to note, however, that while most U.S. corporations see layoffs as an acceptable means of improving the bottom line, firms in Europe and Asia disagree. Business leaders in these countries revert to layoffs only when nothing else works and when the sole alternative left is bankruptcy. In a November 6, 1995 *Newsweek* article entitled "Keep Your Profits" we read, "Tokyo and Bonn are convinced that the American ruthless emphasis on efficiency has social consequences they want no part of."[1] This was said despite the fact that both nations, Japan and Germany, were and still are having economic problems.

While the United States' answer to the question, "What is an economy for?" would be "to raise living standards," most other developed countries would counter with, "to create social stability." While the main job of corporate CEOs in the United States is currently to "do right" by their shareholders and to make Wall Street happy, the main responsibility of Japanese CEOs is to take care of their employees. In most other cultures taking away a person's livelihood or taking away their means of survival and self-improvement is considered disrespectful; in most other cultures it is considered *unethical*. These countries tend to define "the greater good" in terms of *social cohesiveness* while the United States defines it more so in terms of *increased individual wealth*.

And how do we define "the greatest number"? Companies in the United States release more carbon dioxide into the atmosphere than any other country in the world, although we are certainly not the only culprit. The carbon dioxide results from manufacturing processes that keep our economy growing, and that are helping the world economy grow. At the same time, an increasing number of scientists suspect that the carbon dioxide released is the major producer of the "greenhouse effect,"—the global warming that could eventually cause serious environmental damage. Which "greatest number" should we be talking about, today's greatest number or the greatest number making up future generations?

Obviously, those advocating utilitarianism have a lot of hard questions to address. Obviously, defining "the greatest good" and "the greatest number" depends on who you go to for an opinion.

And, obviously, a standard is needed.

The same holds true for egoism. Is there a point at which egoism has to be reined in? Is there a point at which society needs to say, "Okay, enough! You're going too far now! No more!" Adam Smith, the father of modern-day *laissez-faire* economic theory, believed this issue would take care of itself. He said that our "inherent, inner good" would help us define limits and would keep us from exploiting our fellow man.

The early Industrial Revolution proved Smith wrong. It quickly became obvious that when unrestrained by government regulation, many industrialists were capable of anything. They would literally work employees—men, women, and children—to death in order to increase their own wealth. The concept of "the economic man" came into vogue during this period. The most important objective in life was to increase one's wealth using any means available. Wealth came before all else.

The key question with egoism, therefore, is, "Where do we draw the line?" Man has proved himself incapable of handling total economic freedom. Too frequently it is the most neurotic or the most insensitive person who rises to the top and stays there, rather than the most talented and humane. The "robber barons" who shaped the U.S. economy between approximately 1860 and 1910 were a good example of this. When one delves into the private lives of these men we find that most were obsessive and highly paranoid. Their lives were totally dedicated to "winning." Little else mattered.

Because the economic philosophy of the United States during the early Industrial Revolution remained very close to the *laissez-faire* end of the scale and very far away from the socialism end, because the government was weak and had little impact in the economic arena, the individuals in this group were able, literally, to do anything they wanted, ethical or unethical. As a result of their values and intelligence these men eventually gained full control of key industries (banking, steel, coal, railroads, shipping, meat packing, etc.) and used that control to further extend their power. One of the "robber barons," J. P. Morgan, who took over the nation's banking industry, eventually extended his financial power so far that he came close, at one point, to gaining control of the entire U.S. economy.

The private battles that raged between the individual barons sent great economic shock waves rolling through the country. During one of these battles precipitated by Morgan's efforts to add a major transportation system to his holdings, a terrible panic began in the stock exchange that ruined thousands of investors. When asked by a reporter if he felt any responsibility for the situation Morgan replied, "I owe the public nothing."[2]

Another example of this attitude would be the life of Daniel Drew, a key player in the stock market in the 1850s, who considered the honest people of the world to be a pack of fools "who should be taken advantage of whenever possible" and, yet, who was considered a hero by the Wall Street crowd simply because he had made more money than almost anybody else. In one of Drew's best-known exploits, he took control of the Erie Railroad, then drove its capital value up through various market manipulations. As a result, the value of the railroad's stock also rose. At the same time, however, Drew refused to invest in the maintenance or replacement of broken down "rolling stock"—railroad cars, engines, etc. Eventually, due to this neglect a series of horrible accidents occurred costing hundreds of lives. The accidents, in turn, caused the value of Erie Railroad stock to drop. Drew had previously and privately "sold short" his shares so that he profited handsomely from the (pre-planned?) carnage.

UTILITARIANISM FINDS CHAMPIONS

During the Enlightenment Period, which followed the Protestant Reformation, utilitarianism went through a period of radical transformation. It was formalized as a school of ethical thought and its characteristics and applications were properly defined. Jeremy Bentham (1748–1832), a famous lawyer, led the way. Bentham's main interest was in updating Britain's legal system, and in moving the country beyond its feudal roots. However this thinker also ventured into the realm of philosophy. He believed that the definition of right and wrong should not be left to intuition but that it should be the result of a thorough analysis of the individual situation.

Concerning the nature of right, Bentham wrote that utility was the best criteria and that *utility in terms of the whole* should be the standard rather than *utility in terms of the individual*. If this logic was followed, if the whole was "empowered" politically, and if the whole was allowed a voice in decisions affecting it, Bentham believed that the ultimate result would be achievement of the greatest good for the greatest number.

In terms of judging the utility of a decision, he said the decision that provided *the greatest happiness* was the correct one. He also said that the morality of actions must be judged by the consequences they produce, and that happiness for the greatest number is what we should seek. Bentham equated "happiness" with "pleasure." He then developed a means of mathematically calculating the degree of pleasure and pain generated by an action, thus giving us a tool for deciding whether the decision preceding the action was "right" or "wrong."

The philosophical basis for Bentham's concept of utilitarianism was, of course, empiricism. He argued that because a separate judgment had to be made in each situation, based on the degree of pleasure or pain generated, no set code of "right" and "wrong" could be identified. He said that whether a decision should be defined as right or wrong was specific to the individual situation. In Bentham's version of utilitarianism, therefore, scientific research was the key to discovery of the most reasonable answers.

But Bentham also acknowledged the existence of egoism as a powerful and contrary force that needed to be dealt with. He said that the common tendency of man is to make the pursuing of his own self-interest a duty and a virtue, which means that individuals will tend to put the satisfaction of immediate self-interest before the short-term or long-term good of the whole. Bentham said that it is up to the legal community, the religious community, and public opinion to prevent this from happening.

John Stuart Mill (1806–1873), a student of Bentham's, carried the utilitarianism banner forward, made it more palatable, and struggled to find ways to put it into practice in the social arena. Concerning palatability, he discounted Bentham's quantitative approach to the definition of right and wrong, reverting to human reason and the lessons of experience as the appropriate basis for judgment. Concerning the social arena, he supported Bentham's call for government intervention in the economic sector.

Mill served one brief term in Parliament—1865–1868. While there, he introduced the concept of taxing the wealth generated by industry and using the moneys collected to provide services for the general public. Utilitarian reforms proposed by Mill included compulsory education for all, equality for women, birth control, and the public ownership of natural resources.

Chapter 5

Deontology vs. Relativism

SEARCH FOR A CODE OF CONDUCT

The second set of opposed schools of ethical thought we spoke about in a previous chapter includes *deontology* and *relativism*. These concern not *whom* we should focus our attention on when making ethical decisions (ourselves or society) but, rather, *what frame of reference* we should use when making such decisions.

Deontology tries to establish a code of proper conduct based on the rights of the individual. Rather than talking about results, or about who should benefit from an action, it talks about what we should take into account *before* acting. It says there are things we *should* do, and rights we *should* respect regardless of the situation, rights that are "carved in stone" so to speak.

Society has been attempting to spell out the difference between right and wrong since the beginning of civilization. One of the first attempts was a legal code developed by Hammurabi, king of Babylon, between 1955 and 1913 B.C. that was literally carved into a block of black basalt. The Hammurabic Code defined penalties for unjust accusations, false testimony, injustice done by judges, and improper treatment by physicians. It also established laws concerning property and financial transactions.

In terms of modern-day western society and the definitions of right and wrong that have shaped it, the Ten Commandments of Judaism that were later adopted by Christianity are one of the earliest examples of such a document. Eight of these commandments that Jews believe were given from God to Moses begin with "Thou shall not..." They include "Thou shall not kill," "Thou shall not steal," and "Thou shall not bare false witness against thy neighbor." These commandments are an instrument of social control which clearly defines behaviors that are not acceptable and that merit punishment. Even the three commandments that begin with "Thou shall," rather than with "Thou shall not," talk about how people are required to behave—"(Thou shall) honor thy father and thy mother," "Thou shall have no other gods but me," and "(Thou shall) remember and keep the Sabbath day holy." These three commandments define things people are required to do, and assume that if they don't obey they deserve to be punished. The three "Thou shall" commandments, therefore, are also instruments of control.

The deontological school of thought differs in a very important way from the Ten Commandments. Rather than talking about responsibility or about behaviors people *shall* and *shall not* demonstrate this school speaks of the *rights* of the individual, or of what people should be allowed to do. It says activities that infringe on these rights are unacceptable. By focusing on the rights of the individual, on what one *ought* to be allowed to do rather than on what one *shall or shall not* do, deontology becomes a philosophy mainly of *empowerment* rather than one of *control*.

A key question that arises immediately concerning the deontological perspective in ethics is, "What are the criteria for accurately defining individual rights?" Determining these criteria is open to just about any interpretation. Can rights be defined by one person? Karl Marx's definition of economic rights started a revolution. Should rights, instead, be defined by consensus? The United States Congress, a representative body, created the Bill of Rights, which defined the political rights of every citizen.

In the world of philosophy very few attempts at generating an acceptable, generic model for individual rights have stood the test of time. One that has we will call the *political model*. People supporting this model believe that individuals have specific rights including:

- freedom of conscience (freedom to follow one's conscience when defining right and wrong)
- freedom of consent (freedom to say yes or no when asked to do something)
- freedom of privacy
- freedom of speech
- due process (the right to be tried fairly in a court of law)

Of course, giving everybody "freedom of conscience" opens the door to egoism—"My conscience tells me that I should pursue only my own self-interest and not worry about anybody else." In order to respect this right of an egoist, society is forced to put the rights of others at risk which raises the question, "Do I have the right to think solely about myself, and to show no concern for others when I am exercising my freedom of conscience?"

This question, again, can solicit a number of different responses, depending on the person responding.

Next comes the "freedom of consent." According to this right, when an egoist following his freedom of conscience tries to force others to act or to speak in a certain way, the others have the right to say "no." But, then, which freedom should take precedence, the freedom to follow one's own conscience and to force others to do what we think is "right," or the freedom to say "no"? This is not spelled out by the political model and, therefore, opens the door to conflict and to possible injustice. History is full of stories of people who have tried unsuccessfully to say "no."

A second, more indirect generic model for defining individual rights was offered by Emmanuel Kant, the eighteenth-century philosopher discussed earlier. In the field of ethics, Kant developed the *categorical imperative* that says that in order to discern whether an action is ethical (right) or not, one must "act as if the maxim of thy action were to become by the will a universal law of nature." A more easily understood interpretation of this pronouncement might be "act only if you believe that what you intend to do will be acceptable to the rest of the world on a long-term basis."

It is important, however, to notice that I said "*the* world" and not "*your* world." Egoists, as has been said, tend to surround themselves with other egoists, a support group set-up. In their world, therefore, a totally selfish, destructive act might be acceptable, even admired, whereas beyond the confines of their close-knit group it would not.

A third vehicle for defining individual rights is the golden rule of the Judeo-Christian religion, "Do unto others as you would have them do unto you." This means that individuals have the right to expect others to treat *them* well only if they first treat others well.

Despite its simplicity, this vehicle might actually be the best of all. Egoists, while believing they can justifiably ignore the rights of others, do everything possible to protect their own rights. An example would be the previously mentioned robber barons who ran the United States economically and politically during the late 1800s. While they wanted no government regulation interfering with their exploitive activities, and while they preached free enterprise (let nature's law of supply and demand regulate the generation and distribution of wealth) these men at the same time considered it their right to force government to protect their own economic interests against marketplace competition, especially against competition from the more developed European industrial powers. They also forced the government to protect their right to hoard profits against labor's growing demands for a living wage, for a safer workplace, and for a shorter work week.

Egoists by definition demand that others be unselfish. The golden rule, however, if chosen as the core vehicle of a deontological approach to ethics, would make their kind of behavior unacceptable.

Another interesting characteristic of deontology demonstrates the close ties between ethics and philosophy. There are two types of deontologists. "Rule deontologists" believe that the individual rights we have been struggling to define have been around since the beginning of time, that they are generic and never-changing, and that they have only to be discovered (rationalism). "Act deontologists," on the other hand, believe that individual rights can and should be redefined according to the lessons of experience whenever it makes sense (empiricism).

TYING THINGS TOGETHER

A progression can be defined in terms of egoism, utilitarianism, and deontology. Egoism as described previously involves "law-of-the-jungle" or "every-man-for-himself" thinking. It could be related to Sigmund Freud's "Id" stage of human development, where the infant is totally focused on meeting his own needs with no consideration for the needs of others. One can label this type of thinking and behavior in adults "infantile arrest."

Utilitarianism, the second stage in this progression, moves from self-interest to concern for the community as a whole. It concentrates on defining what is best for the greatest number even though the concerns of the minority might have to be sacrificed.

Finally, deontology says that not just the rights of the community majority must be respected, but the rights of each individual in the community must be respected as well. Rather than centering our lives solely around the satisfaction of our own needs with no concern for others and rather than trying to do what is best for the majority even though the minority might be dissatisfied, deontologists believe we must respect the rights of *each member* of our community.

Deontology is obviously the most idealistic of the three schools of ethical thought. Deontology can also be considered the most impractical. How, for example, can a group find a way to respect the rights of every member when individual needs and desires differ or conflict? Deontology can obviously lead to stalemate when disagreements in terms of "following one's conscience" are irresolvable. Deontology's weakness, therefore, is that it provides no means of judging which of the "rights" that must be chosen from in a specific situation is the *most right* or is even the *more right*.

This brings us to *relativism*, partner to deontology in the second pair of opposing schools of ethical thought. Relativists believe that ethical decisions must be made subjectively. They believe such decisions must be made based on each situation and on the participant's previous and current experience.

Of the four approaches to ethical decision-making that we have examined relativism may make the most sense. Relativists consider the beliefs of the people involved and the situation being addressed before reaching the most suitable decision. Relativists try to get group members to find middle ground and to reach a compromise acceptable to all. At the same time the involved decision lasts only as long as the circumstances it is based on. When views of group members shift due to interaction with each other or due to a changing environment, so might the decision.

A real-world example of such a shift is a company that pays kickbacks to win contracts. Paying kickbacks has been an accepted part of business for a long time. However, a new CEO then takes over who believes that kickbacks will eventually hurt the bottom line. At the same time the local newspaper begins publishing a series of articles on kickbacks, naming both givers and receivers. At this point upper-level management decides that the practice of giving kickbacks no longer benefits the company. Thus, it becomes unacceptable. The company stops doing business with firms that demand them.

The lack of constraint found in the relativistic approach is its greatest strength, as well as its weakness. In terms of strength, the lack of constraint obviously makes relativism the most flexible and adaptive of the four systems we have discussed. Relativism "goes with the flow." If the consensus of the involved population is that generating increasing amounts of individual wealth should be the sole purpose of business, then all right, it becomes acceptable for businesses to do anything necessary to generate wealth. In terms of weakness, the lack of constraint found in relativism can also take us farther than we may want to go because it is not coupled with a foundational code of behavior. For example, someone might say "In order to continually increase the amounts of individual wealth, businesses need to clear-cut our forests and to fish out our oceans."

It should be obvious by now that both extremes on the deontology/relativism spectrum can hamper, as well as support individual and societal development. Deontology provides a necessary frame of reference for social interaction. At the same time, however, it can lock people into a system of beliefs that stifles development. In the political model, for example, if everyone has the right to follow her own conscience in whatever direction it leads, the possibility exists that people will spend most of their time arguing, and get very little done. It would be like, as somebody once said, "trying to herd stray cats." A workplace example would be cross-functional organization improvement teams given the right to work on whatever members want. The major problem, or course, would be picking a project or projects everybody is interested in.

Relativists, on the other hand, say that anything goes so long as we can get everybody to agree. Rather than focusing on individual rights and nuances, relativism says that gaining consensus is the key, no matter how we do it. With this in mind, we all know or have read about industrial leaders convincing their followers to move in a direction that was non-beneficial at best, destructive at worst. The previously mentioned Lucent Technologies and Enron episodes are good examples.

Decision-making in such situations tends to be controlled by the strongest person rather than by the wisest. History is full of examples of strong-willed, even fanatical individuals who have done whatever was necessary to gain control, who believed in their hearts that they alone knew what was right for the situation, using this sense of conviction to talk others into believing that their choice was the best before leading followers over a cliff. While the freedom of relativism sounds good, it rarely produces the best results. Personality frequently plays too large a role in the decision-making process.

The obvious need is to find a middle ground where rules exist but do not limit the pursuit of an effective solution, rules that facilitate the quest but also control the excesses of the strong-willed. First, however, we should look more closely at this issue of *personality* that plays such a large role in the decision-making process and try to make sense of it from the perspective of ethics.

DEVELOPING AN ETHICS-BASED PERSONALITY TYPOLOGY

A number of personality typologies are available. Most are based on behavioral factors—whether people are introverted or extroverted, whether they are active or passive, and so on. Most typologies are built around the *actions* of the individual. They help us discover whether a person changes herself to adapt to a situation or tries to change the situation, whether he fights or flees.

The typology offered here is perhaps more "intellectual" than most in that, first, it focuses on the thought processes that occur *before* any action involving an ethical decision is taken and, second, it focuses on the factors included in a decision concerning *what the desired results of that action should be*.

This typology is built on the two previously discussed sets of opposing schools of thought concerning ethical decision-making—egotism and utilitarianism, and deontology and relativism. When these schools are paired up they give us four neat personality types:

1. Egotistical deontologist
2. Egotistical relativist
3. Utilitarian deontologist
4. Utilitarian relativist

Egotistical deontologists in the workplace care only about satisfying their own needs and desires. At the same time, because they follow a strict code of behavior dictated in many cases by their religion, egotistical deontologists outside the workplace feel a responsibility toward society. Most of the previously mentioned robber barons fit into this quadrant. They fervently believed that their God-given responsibility in life was to make as much money as possible, to gain as much power as possible, and to do whatever was necessary to keep others from interfering with their efforts. In this respect they were totally self-centered, and totally egotistical.

At the same time, however, many of the robber barons believed just as fervently that it was their God-given responsibility to help their fellow man. For some reason these individuals were able to separate their workplace lives from their non-workplace lives. *Laissez-faire* economic theory governed their workplace lives. The attitude was "every man for himself." The objective was to win. The welfare of the workers was not a concern. They were seen as numbers. When the operation could be made more efficient, when the bottom line could be improved by erasing some of those numbers, employees were fired.

Outside of the workplace these same robber barons opened soup kitchens to feed the unemployed. They paid for the construction of public libraries and hospitals. They established trade schools and technological institutes to train the next generation of employees. The private lives of these men were governed by a sense of social responsibility that compelled them to give back.

Our modern-day robber barons, who reside mainly in the financial community and in the ranks of grossly over-paid executives, are generally egoists who feel no such compunction and who are governed by no such code of behavior either religious or otherwise. These people fit into the *egotistical relativist* quadrant. Members of this group, like their predecessors, believe they have the right to do whatever is necessary to increase their wealth during working hours. Unlike their predecessors, however, they feel no need to pay anything back. These people are involved in a private competition to see who can put together the largest pile of coins and who can procure the most expensive impression pieces. The effect their antics might have on the outside world is of only secondary concern.

Utilitarian relativists, those inhabiting the third quadrant in our typology, feel concern about the welfare of society as a whole, but are pragmatic in their concern. They are willing to make social sacrifices when the benefits outweigh the costs. For example, in order to generate more electricity to keep the economy healthy, these people might support the use of nuclear power as well as the relaxing of pollution standards. The question here, of course, is again one of definition. Whose definition of "benefit" are we going to accept? And whose definition of "cost"? While the short-term economic benefit of using increasing amounts of nuclear power might be great, the long-term cost in terms of the effect of nuclear waste on the environment might be greater. While cutting pollution standards might increase productivity in the short run, the harm done in the long run might far outweigh the benefits.

A second concern is that while the utilitarian relativist's approach might be considered more flexible, more capable of adapting effectively to the increasing rate of change in the economic and the social environment, the answer these decision-makers come up with might not take into account the opinions of all important *stakeholder groups*. In the highly competitive workplace culture frequently found in the United States a lot of energy is directed toward keeping the opposition from being heard. As a result, opinions that utilitarian relativism depends on for the most appropriate decision might not be voiced. Utilitarian realists, therefore, even if their hearts are right in their desire for social development, have to be careful.

The last quadrant in our typology houses *utilitarian deontologists*. This personality type also has the best interest of society in mind. At the same time, however, it attempts to define universal, individual rights that are important to the shaping of decisions. It believes that by protecting the rights of each and every individual, it will actually be doing what is best for society as a whole. It wants to make sure that everyone is heard and that everyone's needs are met when a decision is finally reached.

The problem facing utilitarian deontologists is obvious. It is basically the same problem facing the deontologists. An example would be the previously mentioned *guilds* that regulated trade during the Middle Ages. Each craft had its own guild and all craftsmen that practiced the trade belonged to it. Due to environmental circumstances, strict regulation was necessary to survival. One of the rules set by the guilds was that any technological innovation developed by a member had to be approved by all other members before it could be used. But such approval rarely materialized. Any innovation or new technique would at least initially give its presenter an advantage. Therefore, most were voted down.

The no-win situation created by this rule, although it was instituted with the best of intentions, obviously slowed progress and discouraged individual initiative. The key to success in terms of utilitarian deontology, therefore, would be to discover a rule or a standard that protected the rights of individuals, while not slowing economic and social progress.

Where do people look for such a rule or standard? This book seems to be asking that question a lot. In fact, the question has been voiced when the weaknesses of each of the four approaches to defining ethical behavior—egoism, utilitarianism, deontology, and relativism—have been discussed. All four perspectives lack adequate boundaries. All four schools of thought lack a focus that makes those boundaries apparent. And to make things worse, the two schools in each pair of perspectives are diametrically opposed while the two pairs themselves come from entirely different realms. The first pair, egoism and utilitarianism, as we have said, comes mainly from the realm of individual beliefs and personality. The second pair, deontology and relativism, comes from the realm of social philosophy.

Obviously, in order to discover the desired rule or standard we first need to find some common ground.

FINDING COMMON GROUND

Our search for common ground must begin by returning to the original two pairs of opposing ethical systems. Each of these pairs, it turns out, can be spanned by a third, more neutral school of thought defined more recently by ethicists.

With egoism and utilitarianism, the spanning school of thought is *enlightened self-interest* developed to counteract the potential harshness of egoism. This more neutral school believes that individuals should pursue their own ends, but that they should do so in ways that do not harm others.

In terms of deontology and relativism, the spanning school of thought is the previously mentioned golden rule school. The golden rule has been defined as one of the "laws" or standards deontologists can choose to construct their reality on. Followers of this school believe they should react to each situation as unique. At the same time, however, they should make sure their reactions do not affect others in ways they themselves would not like to be affected if on the receiving end.

These two bridging schools of ethical thought, *enlightened self-interest* and the *golden rule*, are obviously quite similar. The balance point, where they cross in the diagram, could be considered the ideal, that point where the four original schools of thought combine to make the most sense. It is the point where self-interest and interest in the community as a whole, the point where the need for laws to govern behaviors and the need to allow people to figure things out for themselves come together, blending in a way that incorporates the *strengths* of the four original schools.

Still, how can one be sure? How do we know that this unification does not, instead, incorporate the *weaknesses* of the four original schools, or does not create a situation where the strengths and weaknesses of the four original schools cancel each other out?

Once again it becomes obvious that something is missing in our quest for an effective approach to dealing with ethical issues in the workplace. For that matter it also becomes obvious that something is missing in our quest for an effective approach to dealing with ethical issues in life in general.

This something is, of course, a *standard* that makes sure the strengths from the four original schools are incorporated into the approach and that the weaknesses are excluded.

Chapter 6

Identifying the Standard

THE ONGOING QUEST

So far the discussion has centered around criteria for shaping individual actions—pursuing self-interests, focusing on the good of society as a whole, making ethical judgments based on a set of predefined rights, and doing what makes the most sense in each individual situation. Quite a few sets of criteria obviously exist. What is missing is *a universal standard that aims society in one specific direction and that defines an ultimate objective by which to judge all ethical decisions.* What is missing *is a standard that helps orient self-interest before people act, that helps define what is best for society as a whole, that provides a comprehensive starting point for the definition of ethics-shaping rights, and that provides a reference point to focus on as individuals struggle to adapt to a constantly changing environment, to define the best choice in each situation.*

What is missing is *a generic standard upon which to base all decisions, a standard that will make sense in terms of all possible alternatives.* Some feel that success, the achievement of the desired objective, should be that standard. The pragmatists are in this group. But once again we must ask, "What is *success?*" The egoist's definition of success obviously differs from the utilitarian's definition. The deontologist's definition of success is predetermined, while the relativist's is flexible. And what about the nature of the objective, should that be taken into consideration?

Other people use the concepts of *right* and *wrong* as their standard. But, again, a deontologist's definition of right would obviously differ from a relativist's. Soren Kierkegaard, Frederick Nietzsche, Jean Paul Sartre, and others champions of *existentialism,* a philosophical school of thought that emerged during the nineteenth century and is still popular today, complicated things even further by telling us that no such thing as a right or a wrong ethical decision exists. Existentialism focuses on the uniqueness and isolation of the individual in the universe. It plays down the role of society and societal standards. It says that each individual must passionately define his own standards, but that we must also take responsibility for the consequences of our actions. Nietzsche went so far as to proclaim in his book *Thus Spoke Zarathustra* that "God [as the ultimate judge of morality] is dead." Nietzsche was reacting to a situation in Europe where moral dictates had become so restrictive, so overpowering, so smothering, and at the same time so hypocritical that they had lost their value.

Existentialists say we should spend our time trying to discover what is right for ourselves rather than trying to satisfy the dictates of a corrupted society or trying to understand the dictates of a universe that is purposeless and has no concern whatsoever for its inhabitants. The existentialists say that questions concerning the rightness or wrongness of an action cannot be answered by religion, by reason, or by science because there are no universal answers. No reward exists for doing right; no punishments exist for doing wrong because these concepts are completely arbitrary.

Existentialists say there is only *now*. There is only the moment along with our total freedom to shape it subjectively and passionately. Reality is only what we are capable of personally creating and personally experiencing. If we wait for our environment or for the universe to shape that reality, we will come to nothing.

Finally, Nietzsche said that the only way to measure the value of our actions is through the degree of self-defined greatness and excellence achieved.

Existentialists explain that the concept of universal right was developed by man as a means of giving himself hope, because man has an innate need for order. The existentialists say that man developed the concept of right because we are unable to accept the only real truth, the only available absolute, which is that no order, no meaning, God-given or otherwise, exists in the universe. Existentialists believe that people are truly on their own and that the only reality they can hope to discover is the reality they create individually.

Humanity, of course, has trouble with such pronouncements. We continue our struggle to find something irrefutably true, or something beyond what we ourselves have concocted, or something that makes sense. This dilemma, the fact that we cannot help but struggle knowing that our struggles are hopeless, can be considered a cruel joke, one that turns life into an endless battle we have no chance of winning unless, that is, we refuse to accept our situation and decide consciously to create our own reality, our own meaning.

An extreme example of man's unwillingness to accept the hopelessness of his situation is found in the Greek Myth of Sisyphus by a story about a man who angered the gods and as a result was given the task of rolling a boulder to the top of a hill. The punishment was that every time he almost reached the top the boulder broke free and rolled back down to the bottom, making his task grueling, frustrating, and neverending. Instead of complaining or despairing, however, Sisyphus kept at it. Albert Camus' interpretation of the story is that he did so in defiance of the gods, to show them that while they could force the situation upon him they could not control his reaction to it. By acting in this manner, Sisyphus created his own purpose and his own reality, thus giving his life meaning, thus defeating the gods. The last line of Camus' essay, *The Myth of Sisyphus* reads, "One must imagine Sisyphus happy" because "… his fate belongs to him. The rock is his thing."

The ideas and attitudes proposed by existentialists obviously sound radical. *Nihilism*, a related school of thought revived during about the same period, was even more radical, adding the belief that traditional social institutions—governments, churches, schools—rather than facilitating the creation of our own reality or our own individualized values, impede it. Nihilists believed the main role of these institutions was to force everybody into the same mold or the same mindset, so the population could be more easily controlled. Therefore, such institutions were the enemy of self-discovery. Therefore, they needed to be abolished.

Sounds pretty bad, but we must remember that the original European existentialists and nihilists made their contribution to the world of philosophy during a period when their continent was tearing itself apart, when the old order was collapsing, the old empires were crumbling, the culminating event in this collapse being World War I during which hundreds of thousands of men died gruesome deaths in the trenches, during which one French general boasted that if his armies could keep the casualty trade-off between France and Germany even, the French would eventually win the war because Germany would run out of soldiers first.

Ethics and philosophy are shaped mainly by four things—intelligence, education, intuition, and environment. In the case of the early existentialists, environment obviously played a major role. Life for most Europeans during the late 1800s and early 1900s was bleak and hopeless. There seemed to be no future except endless war and death. The existentialists said, "Yes, this is the way things are and we can do nothing about it." They discussed the indifference of our environment, of a universe that has no connection to us whatsoever, no connection to the tiny specks of life inhabiting it during their brief moment of existence. Existentialists said that we had to accept this indifference and go on about our business.

At the same time, existentialism can be considered extremely humanistic in its focus on the individual, on clearing away obstacles to individual empowerment. Existentialists advocate breaking out of old molds, out of old social orders that have grown too ponderous and creating a new reality, creating an individualized reality based on individualized values.

Most people in modern times like the part about creating their individualized reality. However, they do not like the part about the quest for ultimate truths being hopeless, about the quest for order in the universe being hopeless. While humans want individual freedom, they also want some degree of social order, and such order has to be based on if not *ultimate* truths then at least *consensually agreed upon* truths and standards that allow society to progress and improve.

This has been *the* major theme of human history—societal improvement. Healthy humans possess an innate desire to enhance not only their own fortunes, but society's fortunes as well. Healthy human beings want to make positive contributions that will improve their world. A lot of backsliding has taken place. Human progress never seems to move forward in a straight line. Rather, it moves in loops, pushing a little bit forward, then looping back on itself, the next push forward carrying society out even farther so that improvement continues.

And, of course, existentialism has been extremely popular with the egoists who have little use for universal definitions of right and wrong, who are very much so into creating and defining their own reality. One such egoist, Adolph Hitler, used this philosophy coupled with the concept of the need for social anarchy offered by the nihilists as the rationalization for his destruction of Europe and his attempt to conquer the world.

CLOSER TO HOME

People continue searching for the elusive standard, the one that will give them a common, acceptable focus as they create their individual realities, a standard that will allow individual efforts to facilitate societal development as well. And despite what the existentialists say, such a standard will help individuals differentiate between things that are acceptable and things that are not, between actions that are *right* and actions that are *wrong*.

In the modern-day workplace, on a very simplistic level, many companies believe they have come up with what we are talking about—a standard that we can use to base decisions on. That standard is customer satisfaction. Employees are told to orient their workplace efforts toward satisfying the customer. This objective should help them decide which actions are right and which actions are wrong.

The belief that customer satisfaction qualifies as a universal standard for ethical decisions in the workplace, however, or for any kind of decisions in the workplace, is highly questionable. As a standard it seems too open-ended, and too pragmatic in the dark-side sense. For example, how far should employees go, how far should they be allowed to go in their efforts to satisfy customers? Also, what about the trade-off between short-term and long-term satisfaction? Should companies be willing to cut research and development (R&D) expenses in order to keep prices down and current customers happy when R&D is the key to future satisfaction in a rapidly evolving marketplace? At the same time should companies be willing to sacrifice the quality of their employees' working life in order to satisfy customers? If a customer is unnecessarily rude should a salesperson be forced to smile and accept it?

It must be asked whether customer satisfaction is a reliable standard upon which to base ethical decisions or, rather, *a way to measure the success of the standard eventually chosen.* To me, it is the latter. Customer satisfaction is too limited and unsophisticated to serve as a generic standard just as *laissez-faire* economic theory is too limited and unsophisticated to serve as our social philosophy.

Where, then, if not in the workplace, do we look for a standard upon which to base our ethical decisions? Where do we start our search?

BACK TO THE BEGINNING

The standard sought, if it is to be of value, must be indisputable, one that no-body wants to argue with. The standard must be universal. All four schools of ethical thought must be willing to accept it. Kant's *categorical imperative* has been proposed. In order to design something indisputable, however, Kant was forced to make his offering extremely general. Basically he said, "Do not make decisions that you and others cannot live with in the long term." The political model offered by the deontologists, the second alternative discussed, was too specific. It defined the nature of ethical behavior in specific situations (freedom of privacy, freedom of speech, etc.), providing a different standard for each situation, rather than discovering one that could be applied to all.

Those searching for the elusive standard are usually looking through the wrong end of the telescope. They have started from the farsighted position, from where they are now, in order to define the difference between ethical and unethical behavior. They should begin, instead, where they want to end up in order to produce the best results. *What if we identified the elusive standard as an ideal? What if, rather than getting bogged down in the endless traditional debate over how best to define right and wrong, we begin by idealizing the end state we wanted ethical behavior to lead to?* What if we begin by asking why societies encourage ethical behavior in the first place? Is it to stop crime, to stop injustice, or to stop exploitation? What if we idealized the kind of society we would have if these things were stopped? What if we imagined where the emphasis in such a society would lie?

Currently, I am aware of only one suitable answer to this last question, "…where the emphasis in such a society would lie?" The answer is not new. It is over two thousand years old and, therefore, has stood the test of time. The answer is that if ethical behavior prevailed, people would spend their time *developing and enjoying their positive potential to the fullest possible extent, and would use that potential to improve society as well as themselves.* The answer is currently called *The Development Ethic* and was first offered by Aristotle, Plato's famous student who most likely borrowed from earlier Persian, Jewish, and perhaps even Oriental scholars.

Aristotle said that life has three primary dimensions—"making," "doing," and "knowing." "Making" encompasses the production of things. "Things" in this sense include the material goods necessary for survival as well those required for the satisfaction of desires (things people consider important but can live without).

"Doing," according to Aristotle, involves the quest for moral virtue. He defined *happiness* as man's ultimate pursuit and as the essence of moral virtue. He also said that this pursuit is a selfish one. The individual's efforts are directed toward achieving her own happiness, not the happiness of others. Aristotle, however, argued that man also realizes he cannot succeed in his personal pursuit of happiness without taking into account the happiness of others. He said that members of a society realize their fates are too closely linked for acts of selfishness to not have negative repercussions that will affect themselves as well as others.

Does this statement hold up in the real world? Consider the expenditure of our major individual resource—personal energy. It is true that people who are totally selfish do not waste their energy assisting others. Instead, however, those people expend a great deal of energy protecting themselves from others they have angered. They also expend energy beating their competition or keeping others from progressing. A large percentage of the energy of totally self-centered people, therefore, is wasted in non-developmental activities.

On the other hand, people who assist the developmental pursuits of others quickly realize that it is a two-way street. They realize that they receive energy just as they give it out. Perhaps even more importantly, they realize that when one person's energy combines positively with that of others, new energy is created. The whole becomes more than the sum of its parts. Everybody receives a bonus.

"Knowing" involves the quest for requisite knowledge. Aristotle defined three types of such knowledge—the type of knowledge required to make things, the type of knowledge necessary to reach the appropriate moral decisions in our quest for happiness or moral virtue, and the type of knowledge concerning the nature and process of knowing.

With these key dimensions—making, doing, and knowing—in mind, Aristotle then identified four basic categories of inputs necessary to individual development. The first included the ingredients of *wealth*. Without a certain amount of wealth, man could not afford the material goods and services necessary to the happiness he seeks through development. The second category of inputs included different types of desired *learning*. The third included the *stuff of morality*—those inputs necessary to the achievement of self-respect and the respect of others in society. The fourth category included *inputs that satisfied our aesthetic senses*. All four types of inputs are necessary to achievement in the three key dimensions of life.

Russell Ackoff, one of the key figures in the shaping of modern-day management theory, in his book *On the Nature of Development* refined Aristotle's work, carried it further, and related it to our current situation. He said that development is a *"process in which an individual increases his or her ability and desire to satisfy his or her own needs and those of others."* He said that the balanced pursuit of the four required inputs, "plenty" (wealth), "truth" (learning), "good" (the stuff of morality), and "beauty" (the result of good aesthetics) is necessary to development. He said that an individual never becomes fully developed; an individual can always improve. This is good, Ackoff said, agreeing with the pragmatists, because *it is the process, the pursuit of development itself that is valuable. It is the pursuit itself that gives us what we want, that gives us Aristotle's "happiness." Our victories and our achievements along the way are important. But life itself can be defined as a pursuit. If people have nothing left to pursue, they have no life.*

Ackoff's pursuit of *plenty* involves the quest for means to ensure the steady supply of goods and services necessary to both physical and emotional security. The pursuit of *truth* includes efforts to gain the information, knowledge, and wisdom necessary to the selection and achievement of work and leisure-related objectives. The pursuit of *good* has to do with the desire for assurances that a fair deal will be received and that people will receive credit when it is due and will not be victimized by those with more power. The pursuit of *beauty* concerns the quest for contentment and excitement in life, the contentment resulting from a pleasing, non-threatening work and leisure environment that soothes the senses, and the excitement resulting from the availability of challenge, newness, and adventure that stimulates the senses.

The author has further refined and simplified the development ethic and has come up with the previously offered modification—*the purpose of life is to develop and enjoy our positive human potential to the fullest possible extent*. The role of society in this scenario is to make available the four key inputs necessary to individual development. The individual, in turn, must use his potential to enhance the caliber of the inputs and to help ensure that they are available to others.

MEETING THE CHALLENGE

The major challenge in this scenario has to do with the generation and the distribution of Ackoff's *plenty*. Wealth actually serves three purposes rather than two. The first purpose is helping people gain the things necessary to survival. The second is helping people acquire additional resources requisite to the development of their potential. The third is that wealth also can help individuals gain status ("I have more money than you!"). It allows people to afford the *impression pieces* respected in a *laissez-faire* culture.

In the United States, unfortunately, to much emphasis is on the third purpose—wealth as a status symbol. This circumstance results partially from the lingering *scarcity mentality*. It results also from the pervasive influence of the *advertising sector*. I stood in New York City's Times Square several weeks ago, and as I looked around, I was stunned by the number of advertisements I saw blinking, flashing, talking, beeping, and clamoring for attention. I read recently that the typical U.S. citizen sees more than 1,000 ads daily, ads for things that we *must* acquire if we want to remain socially acceptable, ads for things that cost money.

Concerning *truth*, the key to both individual and societal development is that all citizens receive an equal opportunity to gain education. If people are given that opportunity and succeed, fine. If people are given that opportunity and do not succeed, fine. At least they have been given the chance to discover and realize their potential. The U.S. school system is currently in a state of flux. Should it introduce the voucher system and allow students to pick their school? Should the system be further privatized? Should all private schools be closed?

The one thing clearly understood is that all young students in the United States do not receive an equal educational opportunity. The deciding factor is again wealth. Funds for public schools are not equally distributed as they are in other countries. Rather, each district in the United States supports its own public schools through taxes with wealthier neighborhoods obviously enjoying an advantage.

The same holds true at the college level. In other, more development-oriented cultures, education at this level is free. In the United States a degree from a top private academic institution now costs well over $100,000. Even with financial assistance most people cannot afford that.

Concerning access to *good*, democracy as a system of government provides the best opportunity for the development of individual and societal potential. In any democracy, however, a continuous battle rages between the egoists and the utilitarians. The egoists, or the "old boys," believe their small, successful band is better qualified to make the important decisions than the general public. The utilitarians, on the other hand, struggle to keep the decision-making process participative.

In the workplace, democracy rarely exists. In this arena, the "old boy" mentality holds sway. Russell Ackoff has commented on this very interesting paradox. Citizens in democratic societies understand and appreciate the advantages of their form of government and defend it strongly. At the same time, however, most of the companies in these societies are run as dictatorships or as fascist regimes, where a small group (management in this case) makes all of the decisions. "Why is that?" Ackoff asks. If democracy is the best form of governance for society as a whole, why will it not serve equally as well in the workplace? Do employees mutate when they walk through the company door? Do they lose their power to understand issues, to reason effectively, or to form a consensus?

That is an interesting question.

Concerning *beauty*, everybody seeks it. It can be discovered in the natural world, but it can also be created. Beauty is hard to define. It can be found in an object, in a relationship, or in a private moment. One of the things scholars do know for sure is that beauty has to do with fullness, and that the concept of *fullness* and the concept of *efficiency* do not always walk hand in hand. Increasing the level of efficiency in the world of work has to do with cutting away, with paring down. When parts of things are cut away or when things are pared down, their fullness is frequently destroyed.

Due largely to the modern-day workplace emphasis on efficiency, the input of beauty is the one employees have the least access to. Conscientiously depriving employees of beauty, according to our new standard, is unethical. A growing number of studies have shown that depriving employees of beauty is also counterproductive in terms of the bottom line.

By way of a quick workplace example, when managers chop an office space up into small, uniform cubicles, or when managers say that employees are not allowed to put anything personal on the walls of their cubicle, or when managers say employees should not talk to each other or that employees should ask questions only of their supervisors, then managers are thinking solely in terms of efficiencies, in terms of getting rid of distractions. If the desire is to develop and to benefit from employee potential, however, they are missing the point.

One other input, *time*, has more recently been added to the list. During Aristotle's era finding the time necessary for developmental pursuits was not as much of a challenge as it is today. Without appropriate amounts of free time it does not matter how much of the other key inputs people have access to. They are not able to take advantage of them.

Society in the United States is currently organized so that *a vast majority of the individual's time is spent in the pursuit of plenty*. Truth, good, and beauty are too frequently made subservient to the pursuit of plenty. There is a need for a more balanced approach if society is to achieve the best results in terms of individual and societal development.

REACTION TO THE STANDARD

Using the *development ethic* as a generic standard for the definition of ethical behavior gives an acceptable focus to all four schools of ethical thought, a situation one might have thought impossible to achieve, taking into account the diversity of opinions involved. The *development ethic* does not contradict any of the schools. In fact, it supports all of them in their variety of approaches.

In terms of *egoism*, what can be more important to the individual than the fullest possible development of her positive potential? It is the realization of potential that allows individuals to achieve those things in life deemed the most important—the kind of job desired, promotions, recognition, enjoyment, and self-confidence. It helps people differentiate themselves from the crowd. The hard part for egoists will be the giving back part. If society accepts the *development ethic* as its standard, however, and if in order to be recognized and applauded, people must not only show how good they are individually, but also must make a contribution to society as whole, the egoists will do so.

In terms of *utilitarianism*, the fulfillment of positive individual potential should be the primary objective of any healthy society. Such potential, more than any other resource, is the foundation upon which the society is built. Utilitarians should understand this and accept that the greatest good for the greatest number will be achieved by using the *development ethic* as their standard.

In terms of *deontology*, a frame of reference now exists into which individual rights can be fit. Do these rights help the individual fulfill his positive potential? Do they do so in a manner that does not inhibit the ability of others to do so? Do they do so in a manner that encourages societal development as well? When we look at the political model of deontology and talk about the *right to freedom of conscience*, there are now constraints. Individuals are free to do what is required to develop their potential, but only if the result is going to assist society as well as themselves.

In terms of *relativism*, the standard defines boundaries that people cannot stray beyond in their search for consensus and for the best solution. On the individual side it provides a guiding principle that shapes contributions. On the societal side it encourages the pooling of potential to improve the fortunes of the population as a whole.

The philosopher E. A. Singer said that the ultimate truths rationalists and pragmatists are working continually to discover and achieve should be defined and treated as "ideals" that are always approachable but never attainable. But, once again, is a frame of reference necessary to help identify which truths or which ideals to pursue? For example, can saying that one race, one religion or one level of society should dominate, with all others surviving only in a subservient capacity, be considered an ideal worth pursuing? In the business world, can boards of directors be free to say that maximizing shareholder value is the ideal that companies should pursue no matter what the cost to other stakeholder groups?

It is obviously necessary to set acceptable bounds concerning the definition of our ideals. And, once again, the question arises. "Acceptable to whom?" And, once again, the best possible answer *appears* to be "acceptable to the greatest number." But maybe it is time now to go beyond the greatest number; maybe it is time to define a standard acceptable to *everybody* that *all* ethical decisions must meet.

It should be realized at this point that an important difference exists between the concepts of "ultimate truth" and "standard." An "ultimate truth" is a truth over which people have no control. It is there. It has always been there. It will always be there. It will never change. A "standard," however, is something that people design themselves and accept. The process of designing a standard gives people *control* over their situation, and control is essential to development, both individual and societal.

YES, IT CAN

"Can society find a standard acceptable to everybody that is generic enough to serve as an umbrella for all ethical considerations?" The answer offered by this chapter is, "Yes, it can." With the *development ethic* in place as that standard, and with it governing the pursuit of ideals, the drive of one race, one religion, of one level of society to dominate would obviously be unacceptable. In the world of business, focusing entirely on enhancing the wealth of shareholders with no concern for the welfare of employees also would be unacceptable.

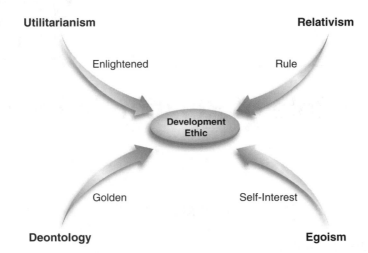

With the new standard in place, the ideals individuals decide to pursue must help them develop their positive potential to the fullest possible extent without hampering the efforts of others to do the same, and in a manner that benefits society as a whole. Such a situation, of course, is impossible to realize as long as the inputs necessary to development are limited or are poorly distributed.

At the same time, no matter what quantity of necessary inputs people might have access to, it is impossible for any individual to fully realize his potential. People must prioritize. Individuals must decide what is most important in terms of the ideal they are pursuing. "Should I study physics tonight? Should I practice the piano? Should I go down to the gym and shoot baskets?" Even if their time was totally their own, individuals would be unable to reach the limits of their ability in all three of these areas—intellectual, artistic, and athletic. They would be forced, eventually, to put most of their effort into just one.

The standard, however, remains of value. The standard *is itself an ideal*, something people work continually toward, but never reach, the benefit coming from the process of working toward it. What has been defined in this chapter, therefore, *is an ideal frame of reference, an ideal standard into which people can fit the lower-level ideals they pursue*. This ideal frame of reference, the *development ethic*, can be considered a *meta-ideal*. Everything else must fit under its umbrella. But now that a standard exists, how do people effectively go about shaping their "lower-level" ideals? This is where previously mentioned *systems thinking* comes into play. Before leaving the realm of theory and values for the realm of application, however, it is necessary to address one more dimension that greatly affects how a workplace society and how society in general approach the issue of ethics. That dimension is religion. It is important to see how our new standard fits with the different schools of thought currently dominant in the world of religion.

Chapter 7

The Role of Religion in Ethics

WHAT IS RELIGION?

Philosophy, ethics, religion, the three are inseparable. None of them can be modified without sending shockwaves racing through the others. The question that needs to be addressed at this point is, "Does religion support the ethical standard just defined? Does religion in its present form support the *development ethic*?"

Answering this question, of course, will not be easy. The first requirement is to decide which religion or religions are being talked about. But even before that, perhaps, it is necessary to develop a clear understanding of what, exactly, religion is and of what purpose it serves in society. Has that purpose remained constant throughout history or has it changed? If so, why? As the major religions evolved, did their belief systems draw closer together? What role has religion played in the workplace historically? What role, if any, does it play today? What role *should* religion play in the workplace and in the definition of workplace ethics?

The question to begin with, however, is the one concerning the purpose of religion in general. The American Heritage Dictionary defines religion as, "*The expression of man's belief in and reverence for a supernatural power recognized as the creator and governor of the universe.*" This definition serves to explain the purpose of religion in modern times. However, it is not complete. Religion has played more than one role on the stage of life, and the growing number of roles it plays have individually become increasingly complex. Religion began as a means of explaining or of rationalizing the many things our earliest ancestors did not understand. It began as a vehicle for appeasing the powerful forces of nature that governed our ancestors' lives, as a vehicle for giving meaning to life and death, and as a vehicle for generating a sense of community.

Almost immediately, those who led the search for answers, the shaman, the priest, and the prophet began gaining power over others, until they also became leaders and decision-makers for their tribes and societies. It is interesting to note that early religious leaders were frequently responsible for dealing with medical, as well as spiritual, problems in an era when people had very little understanding of illness or injury. Thus, in a way, these holy men and women gained influence over life and death. The priest was supposed to possess knowledge nobody else had access to, creating an aura of mysticism around himself and his close followers that led to the belief that religious leaders had developed a link or a channel of communication with a higher power.

Religion provided a vehicle for focusing the masses when other social institutions were not sophisticated enough to do so. It helped bring order to fragmented populations and helped guide humanity into the era of civilization. It provided a unifying force. The other side of this coin, however, in terms of the role religion played, is the old saying that, "Nothing is for free." As time passed, religion as an institution grew increasingly structured and very powerful. It began to dictate not only the nature of the religious rituals necessary for birth, death, mating, planting, and harvesting, but also everyday activities, even everyday thoughts.

This happened for two reasons. First of all, such a level of *control* was initially necessary to help get society organized and to make it safe and productive. The nation of Israel (Judaism is the oldest Western religion) began as a group of wandering, frequently feuding tribes each with its own laws and many with their own gods. The need was to gain control over these tribes and to establish an order that bound them together. The same is true with the nation of Islam. It also began as a group of wandering tribes that eventually were unified under the prophet Mohammed.

Catholicism gained its power in Europe during the Dark Ages, when life was chaotic. The Catholic Church won, frequently through force of arms, increasing amounts of control over the feuding factions, filling the role of centralized government as well as of spiritual leader. The Church helped bring the order and stability necessary to progress. It produced a set of laws, many of them borrowed from Judaism, i.e., the Ten Commandments, to guide citizens in their individual and societal development. The Church also designed the institutions necessary to pass judgment on those who broke the laws, as did Judaism and Islam.

The second, less constructive (at least from this book's perspective) reason religions grew more structured and powerful was that leaders *felt* the need for increasing amounts of control even when such thinking was, perhaps, unmerited. Again, several possible producers of this inclination existed. The first was a sincere belief that without the leader's guidance, people would not think things through well enough, would not control their emotions to a sufficient degree, and would end up hurting both themselves and society. The leaders had the greatest good for the greatest number or for society as a whole in mind (utilitarianism).

A second producer of this mindset in religious leaders had to do with personality. Some people have more need for order and stability in their lives than others. Religion as a profession offered these things. Due to genetics or conditioning, or perhaps to some combination of the two, rabbis, mullahs, and priests took very seriously the laws laid down by their religions (deontology) and saw themselves as enforcers who necessarily policed the activities of their flock to keep members from straying, punishing those who did stray to encourage restraint.

A third possible producer of the need to increase control has to do with egoism. *The chance to be in control of other people's lives offers a great temptation. It generates a feeling of superiority that is hard to resist.* Despite the fact that mullahs and priests and rabbis work to deal with ego issues in training, evidence of strong egoism, including an unwillingness to empower followers, is still sometimes found. This has not occurred in all cases, of course, but it has in enough cases to cause an eventual shift of emphasis from the spiritual toward the political during the history of religion.

HOW IT IS DONE

Three vehicles were and still are used to maintain and increase the type of control and power being discussed. These vehicles are mysticism, a combination of guilt and fear, and the repression or domination of secular education.

Concerning *mysticism*, in Judaism there have been prophets like Moses who possessed a special understanding of what he God wanted and who explained it to followers. However, when something is done that is wrong, each Jew is expected to work things out directly with God. The individual is responsible for making amends. The rabbi is more of a facilitator to the conversation, helping the individual interpret what he hears from God. Rabbis are normal people who have followed a specific course of study, developed counseling, group interaction, communication, and organization skills. They have families. They are respected if they do a good job. They are not respected if they do a bad job. The mysticism found in Judaism is relatively mild. It is found mainly in the Old Testament stories of miracles (the parting of the Red Sea, the burning bush) that helped preserve and make stronger the tribes of Israel. Mysticism is used to help maintain tradition.

In Islam, while Judaic-Christian prophets and biblical stories are accepted, the miracles (the mysticism part) are not as important. Mohammed is Islam's most revered prophet. He lived a normal life, married, and had children. People respect him because God spoke directly to him, reciting the verses of the Koran that Mohammed wrote down. These verses explain in a very detailed manner the way people should live if they want to be blessed and not to go to hell.

Mohammed himself, though obviously blessed, was never considered to have God-like qualities. Of the three religions, Islam has the least inclination toward mysticism. It focuses on the activities of everyday life. In this religion practitioners also talk directly to their God through prayer when asking forgiveness for breaking the laws of the Koran.

The Catholic Church went to the other extreme in terms of mysticism. It picked Jesus as its special prophet. Then it went further than the other religions, elevating him to the rank of the "son of God" and giving him God-like, mystical qualities. Like all other prophets Jesus taught. His most important lessons, however, were offered by way of example: the Crucifixion, driving the merchants from the synagogue on the Sabbath, taking pity on Mary Magdalene. Some of these examples were mystical: the Resurrection, the raising of Lazarus from the dead, the feeding of the multitude.

The Catholic Church then established God's representative on earth, the Pope. The first Pope was the apostle Peter who because of his relationship with Jesus was believed to enjoy a direct connection with God. This connection gave him mystical qualities. One of these qualities was infallibility. God spoke through the Pope. Therefore, all pronouncements made by the Pope were indisputable.

These mystical qualities were passed down through the ages from pope to pope. At the same time, each pope passed some of them (although not infallibility) on to the Church's lesser priests, which were the pope's chosen, thus making them better and wiser than common people. In Catholicism the layman cannot go directly to God to ask forgiveness if that person believes she has done something wrong. Instead, wrongdoers must go to a priest who acts as God's representative, and decides what the person must do to gain forgiveness and grace. This requirement obviously gives the priesthood a large degree of control over the lives of supplicants.

The second vehicle used to maintain and increase control and power, *guilt and fear*, has also historically played a major role in all three religions. In Judaism, guilt results mainly from the scolding and chastisement delivered by other members of the congregation when a person does something that is not considered to be in the best interest of the whole. This person-to-person interaction is a social phenomenon. Jews focus on the here and now, on taking responsibility in this life, and on getting things straightened out in this life. If a Jew believes he has wronged someone else, even though no judge forces him to do so, that person is responsible for going directly to the wronged individual and making amends. Judaism accepts the concept of hell but this concept does not receive the same attention that it does in the other two religions and does not generate the same degree of fear.

In some Islamic societies, religious police (different from civil police who hand out traffic tickets) responsible for patrolling village and city streets in search of those who break the laws of the Koran can assign guilt. Guilt can also be assigned by religious courts (different from civil courts) presided over by clerics. The fear in these societies is of two things. The first is a fear of ending up in hell. The second is a fear of the punishment administered directly by the religious police or designated by the religious court. Because religious law in Islamic nations concerns everyday matters—dress, how one does business, drunkenness, how people handle themselves in public, failure to pray on schedule, the use of profanity—forms of punishment are direct, swift, and usually corporal. They range from verbal reprimands to beatings or whippings to being stoned to having a limb cut off to decapitation.

The Catholic Church also uses guilt and fear as control mechanisms, but its approach is more subtle and less physical. The Church sows the seeds of guilt in the minds of its members at a very young age. They are taught that one is born in sin and is headed for hell if forgiveness is not gained. Catholics spend their lives trying to overcome the guilt planted deep in their psyche. The fear is that they will not be able to do so. Because the priesthood stands between them and God, petitioners are totally dependent on the Church and its representatives to facilitate their quest.

Concerning the *repression or domination of education* as a means of maintaining and increasing a religion's control and power, it is obviously easier to manipulate people when they lack education and when they have to turn to a priest for answers and decisions. History has proven this temptation to be irresistable to the religions being discussed.

Judaism has always stressed the importance of education. However, in traditional Orthodox sects that have grown steadily more rigid the most important subject studied is the Jewish religion. Everything else is secondary and is strongly influenced by religious doctrine. Although men are allowed to pursue advanced education and to become professionals, most of their study time is supposed to be spent reading the three parts of the Tanach, which are the Holy Scriptures. Women, because of their station, are not allowed to seek secular education beyond secondary school. They are not allowed to become professionals, as their place is supposed to be in the home with the children.

Islam, historically, has also valued secular education. In ancient times, many of the greatest libraries and the most productive scholars were found in the Islamic realm. During modern times, however, emphasis in fundamentalist Islamic nations has shifted increasingly toward religious education. Clerics have taken over much of the teaching and have designed the curriculum to meet rigid religious requirements. Female children in some Islamic populations are forced to quit school after only three or four years. In other fundamentalist but less oppressive societies, women are allowed to train professionally, but only in a limited number of fields dealing with social services.

The Catholic Church, in order to reinforce its control and power during the Dark Ages and the Reformation, made any attempt by common people to gain formal education a sin. If commoners had a question they were to go to their priest for the answer. The Church, however, in light of changes that occurred during the Renaissance and the Reformation periods, the invention of the printing press making it almost impossible to limit the distribution of information, was forced to rethink its position. The Church's approach concerning education shifted from denying access toward controlling what was taught, or at least toward influencing what was taught in secular education classes. As a vehicle for accomplishing this objective the Catholic hierarchy developed its own system of parochial school that offered secular education, but secular education laced strongly with religious teachings.

BACKLASH

In their original, traditional form, all three religions—Catholicism, Judaism, Islam—no matter what the approach or the driving motivation, sought to gain control over their followers. In each religion a group of older men became leaders and spent much of their time arguing against change. They did so by interpreting passages from their holy books—the Bible, the Tanach, the Koran—in ways that supported their belief system.

When life is bleak and the general environment offers little opportunity to improve one's situation, people are more willing to give up control over their lives and fate and to follow anyone who offers a means of moving forward, no matter how small the steps. Increasing numbers of people grew increasingly religious—Christians during the Dark Ages, Jews during their ongoing persecution, those practicing Islam during the crumbling of their empire—even when the leaders they followed began to grow increasingly demanding, increasingly harsh, and increasingly intolerant of outsiders. The three religions, although they sprang from similar roots, began warring with each other, first with words and then with weapons, causing the deaths of thousands upon thousands of followers, all in the name of basically the same God.

Catholic leaders announced that people not baptized in the Church would end up in at least purgatory and would stay there until God took mercy on them. Extreme fundamentalist Muslims decided that all outsiders were infidels or "devils" and were destined to end up in hell. Orthodox Jews considered themselves the "chosen race" and wanted as little as possible to do with others including the non-Orthodox of their own religion whom they did not consider to be true Jews. Pogroms, religious wars, and crusades have raged, with the conflicts continuing on into modern times.

There is no way that egoism wasn't and isn't still behind such attitudes and actions. All three religions have some form of the golden rule as a cornerstone of their doctrine. Judaism says, "That which is hurtful to you, do not do to your fellow man." Christianity says, "Do unto others as you would have them do unto you." Islam says, "Let none of you treat his brother in a way he himself would not like to be treated. No one of you is a believer until he loves for his brother what he loves for himself." Leaders of all three religions speak from the pulpit about the need for a more utilitarian, other-oriented, tolerant, and compassionate attitude. Egoism, however, seems to begin creeping in once people get back out onto the street.

It should come as no surprise that many have grown dissatisfied with the performance of these three religions in their traditional form, especially with their continuing need for control and their intolerance. Gradually, dissenters have begun to speak out, to grow stronger, and to gain support. The leaders of the traditional or fundamentalist part of these religions, of course, have fought dissent through the ages trying to stifle it, sometimes simply by killing everyone who voices opposition to their teachings and decisions. But they have failed and, eventually, within each religion a segment emerged that contradicted the traditionalists, and that insisted on taking at least some of the control back.

The reality is that when people lose the right to make decisions, they are losing, per- *haps, the most important part of being alive.* Their chances of gaining self-respect are being diminished. Most important, however, they are losing the opportunity to develop their positive human potential to the fullest possible extent.

Because humans are "purposeful" systems capable of defining their own objectives and, because, as such, they are driven by the desire to develop and enjoy their potential, individuals are going to do everything possible to regain that opportunity. That is exactly what happened. Within Judaism two new groups evolved: Conservative and Reform. The Reform group remains the most relaxed in terms of ritual, mandatory prayer, mandatory dress, and mandatory behavior. Reform Jews control most of their lives and do not pay much attention to the concept of hell as a deterrent. Reform Jews consider a good and advanced secular education for both men and women to be one of life's major objectives.

In Islam, a middle class has evolved that also does not feel the need to strictly follow the rules laid down by fundamentalist leaders. This group also does not feel the need to be disciplined by a fear of hell or by religious police. With middle-class practitioners of Islam, access to an advanced secular education is a major goal for men and women.

Concerning Catholicism, after the church ignored the efforts of reformers during the early 1500s, a portion of the congregation broke away and became Protestants. The major difference between Protestantism and Catholicism is the disappearance of the Pope and of other priests as God's representatives on earth whom people have to go through in order to gain or to regain grace after doing something wrong. Protestants believe that followers should be able to speak directly to God, ministers thus sacrificing some of the control resulting from mysticism.

However, the clergy of this new religion did not want to give up control completely. In early Protestantism there were two major denominations— Lutheranism and Calvinism. Lutheranism did not stray far from the mother Catholic Church in its use of guilt (being born in sin) and of fear (being predestined for hell) as instruments of control.

Calvinism was more extreme. John Calvin was a firm believer in church leadership and control. Like some Islamic societies he used religious police, whom he called his Council of Elders. Members of this force were responsible for watching over neighborhoods, for identifying sinners and for bringing them to the Council for judgment. Sinful behavior included such things as singing, dancing, laughing too loudly, playing cards, quarreling, drinking too much.

John Calvin also introduced the concept of *predestination* that stripped away the opportunity Luther had given for church members to talk directly with God and to influence God's decision as to whether they should go to heaven or hell. Calvin said that God decided before people were born where they were headed and that the decision was non-negotiable. The best people could do if they hoped for any kind on mercy was to lead as righteous a life as possible and to be obedient, with emphasis on the obedience.

Protestantism has always considered secular education extremely important. The Reformation, which birthed the beliefs that divided the Catholic Church, was an economic as well as a religious movement. During the preceding Renaissance the upper classes, i.e., the powerful merchants and Church officials, took most of the wealth generated. The common people wanted greater access to wealth; they wanted to be able to go into business for themselves and to benefit directly from their labors. In order to do so they needed education, they needed to be able to read and to work with numbers.

Martin Luther opened free schools for craftsmen and apprentices to teach them these skills. Eventually, Protestant women were given the same opportunity to learn. The public school system in the United States is a result largely of the influence of Protestant thinking. The exclusion of religious teachings from public school curriculum is also largely a product of that thinking.

The Protestant religion as it matured, however, began to suffer from the same split between fundamentalists and progressives that is found in Islam, Catholicism, and Judaism. The more progressive Protestant groups began to play down the mysticism, as well as the need to inspire guilt and fear. They focused instead on the positive, on making a contribution to society. The more fundamentalist groups did not like what was happening and fought it. They saw the involved change as bad, frequently as the work of the devil, and worried loudly that those turning their backs on guilt would end up in hell.

Concerning education, the fundamentalist Protestant groups in the United States have joined the Catholic Church in its battle to make religious teachings and opinions a more important part of secular education. They seek to break down the legal barriers between religion and public education, and, as an alternative, have started their own schools, where the emphasis can be placed on such religious teachings.

THE OTHER END OF THE SPECTRUM

The more progressive Protestant groups, due largely to the lack of power exercised by clergy over their congregations, have done the most to return control to their followers. An example would be the Unitarian Universalist Church. There is no mysticism here except, perhaps, the belief that God

exists. Original sin and the possibility of going to hell are not a consideration. The church, rather than depending on scripture or doctrine to guide its
members, leaves decisions up to them and gives them control over both their
religious and secular lives. It depends on members' experience, their ability
to reason, and, finally, their conscience to head them in the right direction.

Emphasis in this church is on secular education that serves also as religious education. Such education is delivered in part by ministers and in part
by others, including members of the congregation. Due to the lack of dogma
there is nothing to memorize and very little to discuss that deals strictly with
the religion and not with the outside world as well. Each member of the congregation is responsible for developing her own thoughts concerning the
purpose religion should serve in the world as a whole, the church providing
only very general guidelines for that process. These guidelines include:

1. A belief in tolerance for the ideas of all religions.
2. A belief in the unity of the sacred and the secular because they both
   have their source in the same reality.
3. A belief in the worth and dignity of each human being.
4. A belief in the motivating force of love.
5. A belief in the democratic process, in the need for people to govern
   themselves.
6. A belief in the importance of a religious community to provide support
   as well as positive, constructive criticism.

Notice the difference between these statements and the "Thou shalts"
and the "Thou shalt nots" of traditional religions.

If I were to design a new religion that goes beyond the church just described making the issue of control my major concern, focusing on empowerment of the individual and on supporting that individual's attempts to
realize his potential, it would be even more simple.

There would be no restrictions on who could join. The new religion
would have no dogma. There would be only one law. That would be the
golden rule, "Do unto others as you would have others do unto you." In order
to encourage people to follow its one law, the new religion would stress cooperation in the workplace, in the community, and in the world. It would realize that competition can be fun and can be developmental to a point, but
that the focus must be on cooperation if the best results are to be achieved.

The God worshiped by those joining the new religion would be the same
God everyone else worships. The only thing members would know for sure
is that God wants the best for everybody. There would be no ceremony and
no ritual. Because there are no ceremonies or rituals, there would also be no
formal religious services. The lives of congregation members would be an informal service with people worshiping every minute of every day. A service
in this religion would be an individual or a group of individuals thinking,
talking, and working to improve society.

Prayer would be conversations of the same. Practitioners would not need to direct their prayer upward or downward or sideways, because they would know that God was part of their group and was participating directly. There would be no chants, no mantras, no litanies. Congregation members would believe that God just wants to hear what they have to say. Therefore, communication would be kept as simple, direct, and honest as possible.

The new religion would not be housed in a special building—no churches, cathedrals, synagogues, mosques, or temples. Wherever followers met together would serve as a place of worship, be it on the top of a mountain, in a home, or at work. The people involved would themselves be the sanctuary. Also, this new religion would have no formal leaders and no clergy.

Members of the new religion would not believe in original sin or in hell. Both concepts were developed by traditional religions as vehicles for control. Negative incentives would not be necessary or welcome.

That would be the core of my new religion. It would be built around the desire to give practitioners as much control over their lives as possible and around our ethical standard. I would call this new religion *God's Religion*, or *One of God's Religions*, because it would be just that. It would, of course, tolerate all of God's other religions, converting solely by example.

WHAT ARE THE CHANCES OF CHANGE?

Philosophy, ethics, religion—the three are inseparable. Religion, however, is obviously the most entrenched, the most stubborn in terms of resisting change. While philosophy and ethics are always exploring, always looking for new directions and new answers, religions have barricaded themselves behind centuries of tradition. They offer constancy, which is a thing we all need. However, the price these religions demand for the constancy offered is often too great, hampering both individual and societal development.

Religion began as an institution with a *utilitarian* mission (to explain the unknown and to develop a sense of community). In order to get the congregation under control and organized, however, rules of conduct had to be defined and enforced. Thus, we had *utilitarianism with deontology*. The problem, of course, is that the formulation and enforcement of rules gives power, and power over others appeals to those with a bent toward egoism. So, gradually, the ethical basis of the three major Western religions—Judaism, Islam, Catholicism—shifted from utilitarianism with deontology to *deontology patterned by egoism*.

The shortsightedness and rigidity resulting from this shift precipitated a long period of religious strife, which, at this point in history, society is still dealing with daily. As the level of secular education has improved, however, increasing numbers of people are adopting a more *relativistic* perspective in their religious beliefs, one that balances the need for rules with the growing need for flexibility and tolerance. This more relativistic perspective, in turn, is helping complete the circle. It is moving more progressive sects away from egoism and back toward a more *utilitarian* approach, utilitarianism being defined as a return of control to the congregation.

What is the effect of these changes on modern workplace ethics? Mixed, I would say. Most organization management systems follow the traditional religious model. Bosses answer the question, bosses make the decisions, workers just do what they are told. This circumstance is not a product of chance. Religion is one of the earliest institutional experiences in most people's lives. It is also one of the most long-term experiences, extending nearly from birth to death. Religion is supposed to provide principles and laws to help guide lives. At the same time, however, it provides a model for getting things done, for *managing* an effort whether that effort be running the religious affairs of a community or running a business.

Religion has always played a major role in defining the management culture of businesses. The Catholic Church had much to do with the formation and regulation of guilds during the Dark Ages and Medieval Period. Guild leaders reported to priests on certain matters. During the Reformation, the Protestant Church helped shape management theory with its declaration that hard work was the key to salvation.

With the approach of the Industrial Revolution, religion's direct influence in the workplace began to fade. But the traditional top-down management model *borrowed from the church* remained in vogue. Is this due to the staying power of religion? Is it because this model is planted in minds at a young age so that the traditional church decision-making hierarchy is the first thing employees think of when it comes their turn to shape a management culture?

An interesting question.

No matter what the answer to this question is, however, the top-down management model supported by all three traditional religions and by many of the more progressive ones must, unfortunately, be considered antithetical to our new standard. *It is still about control rather than empowerment.* While leaders of traditional religions might talk about empowerment, their actions line up more closely with the thinking of the egotistical deontologists. They are law-driven and top-down, the major incentives being negative, the focus being on teaching rather than on learning because parishioners cannot be trusted to make their own decisions without strong guidance.

In summation, as a result of these reflections it is hard *not* to come to the conclusion that until the traditional religions either change their ways or lose their followings it will be difficult to make real modifications in organization management systems. It will be difficult to introduce an empowering ethical standard.

8

Exploring the Systems Approach

THE TWIN PILLARS

It is time now to discuss the vehicle that will best facilitate efforts to shape and to implement standard-based ideals in terms of workplace management systems. This vehicle is the *systems approach*.

A "system" is a group of individual parts pursuing a common objective, either self-defined or defined by the system's creator, this quest requiring interdependence and integration of effort if the objective is to be achieved.

The systems approach rests on two pillars. The first of these pillars is the phrase *"A whole is more than the sum of its parts."* The second pillar, as one might guess, is the development ethic. The phrase, "A whole is more than the sum of its parts" was penned by Ludwig von Bertalanffy in the year 1928. Von Bertalanffy began as a biologist, but what he wrote in his book *Modern Theories of Development* eventually affected every science and every endeavor to improve society. Von Bertalanffy's contribution forced change agents to look in two directions at once. The first direction was inward. The systems approach forced people to realize that a system, any system—living, social, mechanical—is more than a collection of parts, that the *interactions between parts* of the system create characteristics none of the parts possess, and that these characteristics help give the system its identity, its purpose, its *strength*.

The second direction is outward. Von Bertalanffy's point was that a system's interaction with the larger system of which it is a part is critical to identifying, defining, and understanding that system. To understand a tree, for example, it is just as important to understand that it provides shelter and fertilizer for plants living beneath it, that it provides food and a home for animals living in its branches, that its leaves breathe in carbon dioxide and convert it to oxygen, as it is to understand the role roots and bark play.

The *systems approach* is a study of the relationships existing between parts of an individual system, of the relationships existing between different systems, and of the relationship existing between a system and the larger system of which it is a part in order to find ways to help that system function more *effectively*. Systems practitioners speak in terms of *effectiveness* rather than *efficiency* because the latter is a strictly quantitative concept and, therefore, is incapable of taking into account non-quantifiable human values, i.e., the need for respect, the need for recognition, courage, love, fear, etc. The concept of effectiveness, in contrast, takes into account efficiencies, but also takes into account the entire spectrum of human values, considering them critical to decisions.

So readers now have not only an approach to making ethical decisions, one that calls for the definition of ideals satisfying a development-oriented standard, but also a powerful vehicle to facilitate the shaping and pursuit of these ideals, that vehicle being the *systems approach*.

When applied to social systems (those including or composed entirely of people) this vehicle requires conscious cooperation. It requires employees in organizations to work together and to support each other's efforts if both the employee and the organization as a whole are to achieve their objectives. But once again the question, "Why do people need to cooperate, why do they need to work together?" arises. When talking about the first pillar of systems theory, "A whole is more than the sum of its parts," this need might be apparent. To generate the unique and necessary characteristics arising from the interaction of a system's parts, these parts must obviously work together. But what about the second pillar—the development ethic pillar? Is cooperation necessary to the development of individual potential? Can people not do this better by themselves, even in the workplace?

The answer to the first of these questions is, "Yes, cooperation most certainly is necessary to the development of individual potential." The answer to the second question is, "No, individuals most certainly cannot pursue development better by themselves, especially in the workplace." Individuals cannot develop their potential to the fullest possible extent, cannot effectively pursue their ideals unless they have been *empowered*. Being "empowered" means that individuals have gained control over decisions affecting them. How does management empower its employees? It does so through *facilitation*, which generates a much more comprehensive form of interaction than *bossism*. Bosses simply tell employees what to do and expect them to obey without question or comment. Facilitators help provide the necessary resources, then encourage employees to decide themselves what needs to be done and how best to do it.

Members of any society feed off each other. They do so either positively or negatively. In the *positive* scenario the members exchange something that all benefit from, usually in the form of data, information, knowledge, or wisdom. But the exchange can also involve goods or currency; it can involve encouragement or sympathy. In the *negative* scenario, only one person is benefiting from the interaction, draining the other person or people. The negative scenario obviously runs contrary to our development ethic standard.

Systemic integration of a social process or of a management process in the workplace, due to its defining characteristic (to get everyone affected involved in making decisions) and due to its developmental nature, avoids the second scenario. The key, then, is to learn how to design our key organization processes so that they are systemic.

Everybody knows of athletic teams loaded with star players that did not perform as well as expected. Everybody also knows of teams composed of non-star players, even mediocre players that performed much better then expected. The difference was that the mediocre players on the mediocre team somehow generated a synergy, developed a mutual support system that encouraged the individuals to play better than they normally would. As a result, the team demonstrated strengths that none of the individual players possess, strengths that arose from the players feeding off of and contributing to each other's efforts.

This should be the situation in the workplace. The major objective of individuals and units should be to do their best and to support each other's efforts. This requirement is not based on altruism. Rather, it is based on common sense and on experience; it is based on the pragmatic realization that in almost all instances, employees and units that cooperate and support each other generate more profit for the company than those that do not.

KEY SYSTEMS CONCEPTS

Key systems concepts support this realization. The previously referred to concept of *openness* teaches people that they can understand the behavior of a system only by taking into account the larger system of which it is a part, as well as the system's internal workings. If people focus on internal challenges alone and lose sight of how the environment is reacting to what they do, or if it is decided that the organization is powerful enough to control its external environment, the organization is headed for trouble.

Keeping an organization truly open to an increasingly turbulent environment requires more than just one or two people paying attention. The best way to do so is to have *everyone* involved, everyone constantly learning from the environment, then pooling and integrating what they have learned in ways that allow the organization to adapt most rapidly.

A second concept supporting Von Bertalanffy's supposition that "A whole is more than the sum of its parts" is the concept of *emergent properties*, also referred to earlier. A company might want to develop a new product. The quickest way to do so is for one person to take charge of the operation, to control the planning effort, and to make all of the decisions. An alternative would be to bring together a group of people with expertise in related fields and to encourage them to bounce their perspectives off each other. One possible outcome of adopting this second alternative is a richer result, something more fully thought out. Another possible outcome is the generation of more than one product, or of a range of products. The process might be slower, or the product or products developed might not reach market as quickly, but the end result will usually be more beneficial to the company and to its long-term bottom line.

The additional richness comes, of course, from interaction of the different perspectives. Process participants learn from each other, adding new input to their arsenal of ideas, reshaping their definition of the challenge and of its possible solutions. When all of this input is dropped into the same pot, when it is stirred and allowed to season itself, a result none of the participants could have reached individually is achieved. The unique part of the result comes, of course, from the interaction. It emerges from the *process* of sharing ideas rather than from the individual ideas themselves. It is an *emergent property*.

A third systems concept is *counter-intuitiveness*. This means that planned change can frequently bring unexpected consequences. An organization must be capable of dealing with those consequences. If the organization is shortsighted or if it sees any deviation from the previously defined plan of action solely as a threat to be reversed as quickly as possible, it is not thinking systemically. *Systems practitioners believe that deviations occur not by accident but for reasons that should be explored* and that, if addressed correctly, deviations can often be turned into opportunities. For this to occur, however, it is important, once again, to involve all those affected.

A fourth systems concept is *equifinality*. This says, simply, that a desired end state can be achieved in different ways and by following different routes. The need is to decide which of these routes is best in terms of things considered important by stakeholders.

A fifth concept, opposite to equifinality, is *multifinality*. This concept says that similar initial conditions can lead to different final states. A system can be designed to produce one result. If the production effort stays open to its environment, however, if it empowers those involved and encourages them to *think*, the same ingredients can produce a variety of results. Two companies built around this concept are 3M and W.L. Gore. Both have been extremely successful. Both began with a single product and expanded from there. They did so by unleashing the potential and the ingenuity of their employees.

A final key systems concept, again previously mentioned, is *purposefulness*. A purposeful system is one capable of defining not only its own needs and desires but also the way it is going to fulfill them. A purposeful system is capable of changing its mind about the nature of its needs and desires and of redefining them. A purposeful system is also capable of changing its mind about how it is going to fulfill its needs and desires, whether they are the originals or the newly defined ones.

The concept of purposefulness is extremely important in relation to the evolution of management philosophy. The earliest companies in modern Western history, those that evolved mainly during the previously discussed Medieval Period, produced basic crafts—shoes, tables, glassware, clothing.

They were small, including the owner and perhaps another "master crafts-man," one or two junior craftsmen or "journeymen," and one or two appren-tices. Companies were usually located in the owner's home or shed. Employees were treated like family members, eating and sometimes even sleeping where they worked.

As companies grew, things changed. With the advent of the *profit motive* and the *scarcity mentality* during the Renaissance, the family mentality disap-peared. The objective was now to get as much production out of employees for as little pay as possible. This drive toward increased efficiency was legit-imized by Sir Isaac Newton's revelation that the universe was a gigantic clock, a gigantic machine created to do God's work. If this was the case with the universe, then a company existing as part of that universe could also be defined as a machine, but one created to do the owner's work and to serve the owner's purpose.

Companies during this period, therefore, could be defined as *purposive* rather than *purposeful* systems, in that the owner gave them their purpose. The machines in these companies were also obviously purposive, their pur-pose having been designed into them. Because workers served these ma-chines and functioned as extensions of these machines, it was easy and convenient for owners to begin viewing them as another set of wheels, gears, and cogs, thus making them purposive as well. Workers lost their human-ness. They lost any remaining control over their work lives. The purpose given to them by the owner was to function as efficiently as possible. Salary was the input, the electricity that supposedly drove them.

This situation lasted until businesses grew too large, too complex, and too expensive for one person to make all of the important decisions. The ad-vent of public ownership (shareholders, boards of directors, professional managers) brought with it the need for companies to begin defining their purpose internally instead of having it dictated by an owner. Boards of di-rectors were given this responsibility along with top-level executives. The employees, however, in this new scenario were still treated like machine parts programmed to do what they were told to do.

It was not until the birth of the *human relations school* of thought in the mid-1900s that industrialists began to remember that employees have needs and desires other than salary, and to realize that when these needs and de-sires are met, employees tend to be more productive. At this point in history, mainly during the last half of the twentieth century in the United States, in-creasing numbers of workers were allowed to become *purposeful* so that the business community now contained purposeful systems (employees) work-ing in companies that were purposeful systems, the companies, in turn, being influenced by an environment containing other purposeful systems.

The major challenge currently confronting systems thinkers in the realm of management theory is how to successfully merge these three levels of pur-poseful systems successfully.

THE ROLE OF WORK IN THE MODERN WORLD

Before attempting to redesign work, however, in that way which most effectively merges the three level of purpose, it is necessary to come up with a definition of the *role of work* that makes sense in terms of the systems paradigm.

Originally the sole purpose of work was to allow *survival*. Our earliest ancestors worked continually to meet their primary physical needs—food, water, shelter, warmth, protection from predators. They had time for little else. As society progressed and as technology advanced, emphasis switched from simply surviving to *improving one's situation*. While opportunity grew, however, so did competition for the most necessary resource—wealth. Control was the key in this competition. The more control owners and managers enjoyed over the workforce, the better the chance (or so they thought) of increasing their share of the wealth generated. The characteristics of our traditional management system—up and down communication, hierarchical decision-making, limited access to information for lower-level employees, evaluation and reward systems that forced employees to compete—resulted in part from a desire to strengthen management's control.

A goal of the systems approach is to reverse this trend. Systems thinkers argue that such an arrangement wastes a large part of employee potential, and that while such waste might have been acceptable during earlier times when less competition existed, it no longer works.

The companies that are currently winning and will continue to win in the international as well as the local economic arenas are the companies that work hardest to develop the potential of all employees and to utilize that potential in the most effective manner in terms of achieving organization objectives. Period.

Well, not quite "period" because there is more. In order to develop a truly comprehensive definition of work it must be looked at from a societal as well as an individual perspective. Work is one of the key pastimes of any society, along with tending to family, gaining education, and participating in government. The purpose of work in terms of society is to generate resources critical to the support of that society including wealth, education, food, health care, and transportation. The purpose of these goods and services is to improve the quality of life.

It follows that the more a society can draw out the potential of its citizens, the better off it will be. *A systemic definition of the role of work in a society, therefore, is that work encourages the fullest possible utilization of citizen potential in efforts to continually improve the quality of life for everyone.* When a society loses sight of this objective, the society suffers. A balance has to emerge between the desire to improve one's individual situation and the desire to improve the situation of society as a whole. Historically, this balance has swung back and forth. To find the equilibrium point is impossible, for it shifts continually, a multitude of cultural factors bombarding it.

What *is* known for sure, however, is that neither extreme is desirable. The extreme of self-interest leads to a pure *laissez-faire* approach, the perils of which will be visited again in the next chapter. The extreme of focusing on society as a whole to the total exclusion of individual self-interest was tried during the era of communism in Russia, China, Cuba, and Eastern European countries. It also failed miserably because it killed individual incentive, and, as everybody knows, there is no development, individual or societal, without incentive.

This leads back to the systems perspective. *Rather than an "either-or" attitude, the systems perspective moves toward a synthesis, toward an "and" attitude that benefits the individual and society simultaneously.* In the world of work, the systems approach creates the type of organization most capable of meeting the needs and desires of the individual employee, the owner(s), and society at the same time; it creates the type of organization most capable of handling an increasingly turbulent environment, an organization designed to learn constantly from that environment and to adapt rapidly so that both the individual and society can benefit.

CHARACTERISTICS OF SYSTEMIC ORGANIZATIONS

Systemic organizations possess four key characteristics. First, as has been said in numerous places, they are participative. They are not *partially* participative. They are *truly* participative. This means that *all* employees at *all* levels have input into *all* decisions that will affect them directly. It also means that *all* employees are given the authority to make decisions and improvements in their own areas of expertise.

Henry Ford, founder of the Ford Motor Company, is an example of a brilliant man who basically did it on his own and made a serious contribution to society as a result. Mr. Ford, however, was a pioneer in a relatively unsophisticated market. As the involved product matured and as the number of competitors grew, he lost his advantage due to his unwillingness to share control over shaping the future of his company with other key stakeholders.

The Henry Ford story is classic in this respect. Mr. Ford's focus was totally on price and on reaching a growing percentage of the market with an affordable vehicle. The key to lowering price was mass production and mass production, by definition, involves grinding out the exact same piece or the exact same car over and over and over, continually striving to make the process and the technology involved more efficient. The essence of this attitude was portrayed by Mr. Ford's famous statement, "Give them any color [car] they want so long as it is black." He did not wish to deal with the inefficiency and the additional expense of adding more colors to the production process.

The people at General Motors, however, under the leadership of Alfred Sloan worked more as a team. With a better understanding of the systemic concepts of *openness, equifinality,* and *multifinality,* they designed their production process to be more flexible. This management team sensed the public's growing desire for diversity and reacted to it by offering a variety of models. As a result, General Motors took over leadership in the automotive industry.

The point is that due to the rapidly increasing complexity of our environment, the possibility of one person being able to keep up with all the changes that might affect key decisions is growing increasingly remote. Emphasis, at this point, must be on encouraging effective participation. It must be on developing communication and decision-making systems that facilitate the most effective utilization of employee expertise on an organization-wide basis. A whole is *more* than the sum of its parts. In order to achieve the "more" we first need to link the parts effectively. Only then can *emergent properties* be generated. Systems theories, methodology, and tools are designed to help us do this.

The second key characteristic of systemic organizations is that they are integrated on an organization-wide basis. This is not just up-and-down, but all-over-at-once integration. Organizational activities must support and enhance each other. Employees on all levels need to understand how what they do contributes to the whole. In order for this to occur, direct access to anyone employees need input from is required.

The third key characteristic is that systemic organizations are designed to deal with constant change. Maintaining the status quo is no longer an option. This characteristic results from the realization that *when we reach the top of the hill, unless we find another higher hill to climb the only direction we have to go in is down.* Systemic organizations are designed to encourage employees to constantly seek ways to improve current products, manufacturing and service delivery processes, management systems, and the work environment.

The fourth key characteristic of systemic organizations is that they encourage continual employee learning. If all employees have been given authority to make decisions in their area of expertise, if all must have a say in shaping changes that affect them directly, if employees need to understand how they fit into the whole and how to integrate their efforts in the most effective manner, if the need for participative, integrated improvement is continual, then the need for ongoing learning is obvious. The better employees are educated and trained, the more valuable their contribution will be. It is a "win-win" situation. The company provides the resources that enable and encourage employees to learn. The employees, in turn, use what they have learned to help the company define, design, and reach its objectives.

THE TIE-IN BETWEEN SYSTEMS THEORY AND ETHICS

The systems approach leads to ethical behavior. Most unethical acts in the workplace are committed either "in the dark," when somebody has information they believe nobody else has access to, or when people believe they are above reproach.

The chances of any of these situations arising decreases greatly when an organization is truly participative or when employees have truly been empowered. It is harder to keep secrets when your fellow workers have access to anyone they need for information. It is harder to keep secrets when everyone is involved in decisions that will affect them. Integration, of course, also limits the chance of someone committing an unethical act without others finding out, as does the concept of openness, because there are now so many pairs of eyes watching.

Concerning the second pillar of systems theory, when companies make the development ethic a cornerstone of their operation, when they treat employees as purposeful systems and try to meet their needs and desires, loyalty is generated. As was said before, a vast majority of employees do not want to behave unethically. If the company treats them decently, they won't. Also, because of the participative and integrated culture produced by the systems approach, employees will be more prone to notice the unethical behavior of others, will be more prone to intervene.

With this in mind, the last part of the book will offer systemic redesigns of key organization processes that help make unethical behavior unnecessary and undesirable. Before beginning the design effort, however, it is necessary to explore one more factor in the general environment that greatly influences society's approach to ethics in the workplace. The first such factor discussed was religion. The second will be the aforementioned *laissez-faire approach to economic development*.

The Legacy of *Laissez-Faire* Economics

A MAJOR HAPPENING

The concept of *laissez-faire* economics was developed by Adam Smith, a Scottish academician, during the second half of the eighteenth century. This was during the Enlightenment Period, a time of great advances in just about every area of human endeavor. The thinkers of this period believed that with the help of science, they could eventually understand all there was to understand about the world they lived in.

The previously mentioned Sir Isaac Newton, a British mathematician, along with Gottfried Leibniz, a German lawyer and philosopher, set the stage for this movement with their development of calculus, which gave scientists a tool for defining the laws that regulated the movement of heavenly bodies. Based on his work and discoveries, Newton went on to say that the workings of the universe were not random, but were controlled by the laws of physics. He said that once we understood these laws we could understand how the universe operated. It followed then that if scientific laws governed the universe, scientific laws also governed systems contained within the universe, and the best way to understand these systems was to discover the involved laws.

Almost every realm was explored—species evolution, city planning, education, politics, climatology, social welfare, agriculture, government, art. Adam Smith made his contribution in the field of economics. He was greatly influenced by the *physiocratic school of philosophical thought* popular in Europe during that period. The physiocratic school built its economic doctrine on a belief in the supremacy of natural law, of order, and of wealth. Smith discovered a natural law that he believed governed the economic realm—*the law of supply and demand*. An explanation of his discovery and the effect this law had on economies was published in his 1776 book entitled, *An Inquiry Into the Nature and Causes of the Wealth of Nations*.

Smith said that an economic system worked best when unregulated, when man did not tamper with nature's law. He said that government meddling only disrupted the natural flow, decreasing the ability of the system to provide the greatest good for the greatest number. This sounds like utilitarianism, doesn't it? Actually, Smith could be compared to Emmanuel Kant. While Kant tried to arrange the first marriage between the *rationalist* and *empiricist* schools of philosophical thought, Smith's work, intentionally or unintentionally, coupled *egoism* and *utilitarianism* in the world of workplace ethics. Smith said that *the best way to generate the greatest economic good for the greatest number was to encourage each individual to pursue his own self-interest whole-heartedly. The law of supply and demand would enter at this point, ensuring that resources were expended in the most efficient manner, producing the greatest benefit for society.*

The law of supply and demand says that price is determined by availability. When only one company is making widgets, which become popular so that a shortage exists, customers should be willing to pay more for them. As a result, both price and the amount of profit go up. But then, naturally, as the word spreads, more companies start producing and selling widgets, which increases the supply until, eventually, supply equals demand, and then exceeds it. In order to continue selling widgets once competition has materialized, producers will begin reducing their price. As the price continues to drop, fewer, then no new companies will join the widget market. Eventually, some of those already in the market will stop manufacturing widgets. As more and more competitors drop out, supply will continue to drop until, once again, demand outstrips supply and the price starts to rise … and so on.

It makes sense. Smith said that if society keeps its hands off, the economy will regulate itself more efficiently than the government could ever hope to. When asked about the possibility of exploitation due to the absence of regulation, Smith said the "invisible hand" would ensure that the individual pursuit of wealth ends up benefiting the whole. But Smith also said that for the supply and demand approach to work, everybody must be willing to play by the rules. Companies cannot, for example, decrease prices artificially in order to force smaller competitors who are unable to follow suit out of business. Companies cannot, for example, build monopolies. They cannot gain control of critical resources and deny other widget makers access. They cannot spread false rumors about the quality of other companies' widgets. Manufacturers have to do their best to win and to add to their wealth simply by raising or lowering their price according to the law of supply and demand. No cheating allowed.

It must be remembered that in Adam Smith's time, most governments were monarchies whose major role was to protect and to subsidize the interests of the nobility, of the rich and powerful through taxes. With his theory, Smith was trying to free up the small farmer and the small craftsman from government constraints and taxes so they could compete in the market and improve their lot while, at the same time, contributing more to society.

The temptation to not play by the rules, however, was too great. Despite the lessons taught by the American Revolutionary War (1776) and the French

Revolution (1787), both of which resulted in large part from the unwillingness or inability of monarchs to follow Smith's council, very few if any of the new, hungry industrial entrepreneurs listened to this second part of Smith's message, i.e., the part about playing fair. Instead, they began doing everything possible to pervert the law of supply and demand in ways that would give them an advantage and would make them the new ruling class. Their exploits turned the early Industrial Revolution in Europe (1800–1850) and the United States (1860–1910) into one of the bleakest periods in the history of human exploitation.

Unfortunately, or fortunately, we learned very quickly during the Industrial Revolution that an unchaperoned marriage between *egoism* and *utilitarianism* in a culture where the *scarcity mentality* colors most decisions does not work. The prize is too attractive. Egoism quickly becomes the dominant partner in the union. The common good is all but forgotten. This arrangement, unrestrained, ends up benefiting only the strongest, or, perhaps, the most ruthless.

It also should be obvious that while *laissez-faire* as an economic perspective and egoism as an ethical perspective compliment each other, critical differences exist. First, as has been said, the ultimate objective of the *laissez-faire* approach is to serve the common good. Egoism, on the other hand, remains totally fixated on improving the situation of the individual. Second, while those with a *laissez-faire* mind-set might understand the value of cooperation in terms of improving their own fortune, egoists, by definition, feel that the only way to "win" is to beat everybody else on the block. While those with a *laissez-faire* mind-set might realize they will benefit the most individually by working as part of a team and by sharing the rewards, egoists immediately begin trying to figure out how to beat their fellow team members and how to take as much of the reward as possible.

Third, egoism generates a short-term perspective. Egoists need to win every little battle, progressing from moment to moment while the *laissez-faire* perspective can be more long-term. For example, "My self-interest will be best served by *not* laying off ten percent of the workforce this quarter in order to earn my bonus. When the market responds, the employee expertise and loyalty saved will probably pay much larger dividends."

CARRYING THE BANNER FORWARD

In the modern-day workplace, egotistical top-level managers are common. We read about them almost daily in the newspapers. In the ranks of middle and lower-level management, people focused entirely on their own success with little regard for that of their peers are also frequently found.

This group has been labeled the "hotdogs."

The hotdogs cannot be missed. An example would be Jake, an up-and-coming young executive with a major truck manufacturing firm. Jake was recently given responsibility for leading the organization's quality improvement process. Immediately, Jake made himself the link between the quality teams and upper-level management. All team accomplishments and failures had to be reported to him. The accomplishments he would carry personally to his bosses, taking credit for them. Concerning failures, he would decide who should be saddled with the blame. Jake was constantly in front of audiences applauding the quality improvement effort. He was constantly making very visible decisions. Jake soaked up as much credit and recognition as he could from the process, then, when it began to falter due to poor design and flagging employee commitment, he hurried off to his next assignment leaving the mess for his successor to deal with.

Jake was a *corporate* hotdog. However, these people are found in every type of organization. While they have been given a variety of names including "pole-climber" and "butt-kisser," this book shall refer to them as "hotdogs" in honor of the immortal *Coney Island Hot Dog*, which drips with mustard, relish, onions, and sauce, but upon closer inspection, contains little meat. It cannot be said that hotdogs are not hard workers. They spend long hours on the job. They will do just about anything, sacrifice just about anything or anyone to advance their careers. They are involved in everything, forcing their way into the lead if possible. They love to give speeches and to be in the spotlight. They are very good at stringing all the right buzzwords together. They never take chances; they never say anything that might raise their superiors' eyebrows. They are the consummate "yes" men and women.

But that's not the major concern. That can be lived with. The major concern is the way hotdogs treat their peers (competitors for advancement), and especially the way they treat their subordinates. Life to them is one fierce competition. They do whatever is necessary to win. Peers are perceived as the enemy. Those reporting to a hotdog are viewed as part of the hotdog's ammunition, to be expended as seen fit in his battles with peers. Lower-level employees are never considered a responsibility. Hotdogs, for example, are very good at downsizing. They are frequently the ones to suggest downsizing staff as a solution, and frequently volunteer to be the hatchet woman, the bearer of bad tidings. This role enhances their feeling of power over others, while proving to superiors that they are a "company person" willing to take on the hard assignments.

On the day-to-day level, hotdogs, while polished in appearance and manner, while usually smiling, are extremely demanding. They tend to manage by intimidation. They love to pull subordinates aside and voice earnestly their concern that the subordinates are not team players. Hotdogs are also very good at lowering the carrot and promising whatever is convenient at the moment with no intention of following through.

A second major concern is that hotdogs, in the current workplace environment, tend to succeed. They are excellent at ferreting out what upper-level management wants to hear and offering it instead of telling the truth about a situation. The task of telling the truth is left to others, the hotdog remaining neutral, watching carefully, taking as much credit as possible when things work out. Once hotdogs have forged ahead of the pack, they immediately begin getting rid of those seen as threats. Hotdogs obviously make many enemies on the way up. All those considered suspicious are dismissed. Into those vacant positions are put people who have proven their loyalty over the years, as well as other hotdogs who are easier to deal with. Those with real expertise and good ideas are kept in their positions to be milked; the hotdog boss ends up receiving most of the credit for their work. Those who prove to be of value to the hotdog's career are not allowed to advance or to transfer out of the department.

Hotdogs work their way up the modern-day organization ladder until they reach the point at which they are home-free, the point at which their smoke screen becomes impenetrable. Now they control their own activities and can keep a sizable number of people jumping through hoops so that the mirage of tremendous productivity is maintained.

PSYCHOLOGICAL ROOTS

Where does this workplace minority come from that represents the purely egotistical attitude, that represents the corrupted *laissez-faire* approach to improving society, that has such a devastating effect on morale and productivity? Where does this "acute egoism" come from? A psychological theory concerning its source is based on human developmental stages. What we are talking about can be labeled *adolescent arrest*. In Chapter 5 the concept of *infantile arrest* was introduced. Some of this probably comes into play as well. Perhaps adolescent arrest is just a more advanced stage of *infantile arrest*, the basic, underlying problem being an inability to see beyond one's selfish interests, to see beyond one's own needs.

Adolescence in the animal world is frequently a period of testing, of competition and, sometimes, of conflict. Young animals moving toward adulthood test themselves against each other and against adults (especially their parents) to discover and hone their strengths, to discover and work on their weaknesses, to see how they fit into the pack, the herd, the group, and the society. Healthy individuals, of course, eventually develop enough of a self-image, eventually feel comfortable enough with their role in society to stop butting heads. They are able to focus more on self-improvement than on defeating each other.

E. H. Erickson describes the involved transition as "achieving a sense of oneself as a whole person ... understanding something of the significance of being a human being amongst other human beings."[1] In terms of Abraham Maslow's famous "hierarchy of needs" we are talking about the fourth-level need to gain *esteem*, which "leads to feelings of self-confidence, self-worth, strength, capability and adequacy, of being useful and necessary in the world." Maslow said that, " … the thwarting of these needs, however, produces feelings of inferiority, of weakness and of helplessness. These feelings, in turn, give rise to either basic discouragement or else compensatory or neurotic behavior."[2]

Those successful in working through level four of Maslow's hierarchy of needs move on to level five, which focuses on the quest for *self-actualization*. Activities at level five are generally more peaceful and more cooperative. Those who get stuck at level four, however, frequently become hotdogs and spend the rest of their lives trying to beat everybody they come into contact with. At the same time, because most people eventually mature and move on to a more cooperative stage and because cooperation involves *giving* as well as *taking*, those who remain stuck in their quest for esteem (who suffer from *adolescent arrest*), enjoy an advantage. They see the willingness of others to give as a weakness to be exploited. Their simplest ploy is to become a friend and to spend dedicated amounts of time finding out what one has to offer that might be of value. They work to find out whether or not one poses any sort of threat. Once the desired information is gathered, the hotdog acts on it ruthlessly and without hesitation.

The problem is that when cooperation goes up against conflict, even against competition, cooperation usually gets creamed. This is a major reason that most of our organization improvement efforts fail. Employees are told they need to cooperate with each other in order to generate the greatest good for the greatest number. Those who take the challenge seriously, however, often get misused by the hotdogs and grow cynical, or even scared.

Hotdogs, then, are an example of what an egoism-based management philosophy leads to and encourages in the workplace. With that said, however, it is necessary to stop and remember that *the human ego as a force is here to stay. Despite the problems it causes the ego is a necessary part of our makeup. Without the desire to prove oneself capable of making a noteworthy contribution, without the desire to perform feats that draw attention and applause, society would not have progressed this far this fast. The ego is critical to societal as well as to individual development.* This is, in large part, why egoism has gained the status of a major school of ethical thought.

But even so, even after realizing the value of and the need for ego as a creative force, the question, "Is behavior driven to the extreme by egoism ethical? Is it right to behave in this manner in the workplace?" must be asked.

If the *development ethic* is accepted as society's standard, egoism is unacceptable. It does not take anyone else into account. Egoism gathers unto itself as much plenty, truth, good, and beauty as possible, but frequently works, at the same time, to cut off or to restrict the amounts available to others. Egoism, more than the three other schools of ethical thought we have discussed, is driven by the *scarcity mentality*. Egoists think mainly in win-lose terms.

A majority of employees have a hard time working with egoists and with hotdogs. Despite their drive, people with this type of personality usually end up doing more harm than good, which leads to the next question. "If, in the long run, such behavior is counterproductive, why is it allowed to continue?" or even more important, "Why is there so much of it floating around?"

These questions bring us back to the central theme of *Ethics in the Workplace: A Systems Perspective*. What if, in most cases, it is not actually the individual employee, hotdog or not, who is causing or exacerbating the problem? What if workplace circumstances are forcing people to behave in this manner? What if the processes that shape workplace behavior are pushing employees toward egoism? In such a situation can or should employees still be held responsible?

In sum, *is it possible that the modern-day workplace culture actually foments and encourages acute egoism*? And, if so, why does it do so?

SAY IT AIN'T SO, JOE

I, for one, believe that the typical workplace culture in the United States *does*, indeed, encourage egoism and that in many cases it actually forces egoism. The proof is that once we get beyond the relatively small group of employees suffering from adolescent arrest one finds a much larger group, maybe even a majority for whom the balance is tipped sharply toward doing what is best for themselves, even to the detriment of peers, even to the detriment of the organization as a whole.

But this does not make sense in light of the argument that the current workplace trend is toward teamwork because a team effort is usually more productive and profitable for both employees and the company. Everybody knows that egoism and teamwork are antithetical and that they do not fit well together. So why the ongoing egoism? What continues to drive employees toward it? The part of the problem that dwells within the employee herself has already been talked about. Now it is time to explore the other part, the part that finds its source in the organization, in its systems and in its culture.

Actually, on the organization side, there is not just one producer. Rather, there exists a system of intertwined producers. Eventually, several key parts of this system shall be addressed. Right now, however, the focus shall be on the one producer that most seriously affects employee attitudes and, eventually, employee ethics.

What is that producer? You might be surprised.

To start off, it is necessary to talk about life in general. It is necessary to talk about what individuals are willing to be selfish about, what individuals are willing to compete for. I have asked this question in every graduate class I've taught for about twenty years now. Most answers begin with, "Enough money."

I ask, "Enough money to do what?"

The answer that eventually comes back is, "Enough money to be secure and to do what I want with my life."

I then ask, "What else?"

The next thing mentioned is usually access to educations in fields students have interest in. After that things like the ability to travel or an active family life are added.

Nothing unreasonable.

After finishing this list, I turn to the workplace. I start a list for the workplace. What are employees willing to be selfish about, what are employees willing to compete for in the workplace? Salary increases and promotions are usually the first two things mentioned. But after that most discussions center on *challenge*. The thing people want most from the workplace in modern times is challenge, the chance to develop and use their potential and the chance to gain recognition for their achievements.

All of the above eventually boils down to, "*What I want from both life in general and the workplace is the opportunity to develop and enjoy my positive potential and to benefit from this development in ways important to me. Also, I want to be able to facilitate the development of those important to me.*"

Sounds very normal and healthy. I do not believe there are many people who would disagree. The next question, however, is, "Must people become egotistical in order to achieve this? Must they be egoists in order to develop and enjoy their positive potential, especially in the workplace?" The answer should be, "No, not under reasonable circumstances."

A major part of the problem and a major reason that people are forced to act in an egotistical manner, especially during working hours, has to do with the lack of personal *time* mentioned in Chapter 6. As we have said, an individual can have access to all the resources required for individual development—wealth, educational opportunity, leaders who facilitate rather than boss, and a environment that both stimulates and soothes. But if that person lacks the *time* to take advantage of what is available, all is for naught.

In the United States a serious shortage of personal time, of developmental time, of family time exists. Estimates of the number of hours spent weekly by the average U.S. employee at work range from fifty to sixty. At the same time, a majority of two-parent families have both parents working. At the same time, a great percentage of high-school kids in the United States find after-school jobs once they are old enough to work.

Fifty to sixty hours per week equals ten to twelve hours per day in a five-day work week; nine to ten hours per day in a six-day workweek. This boils down to not much time for anything else. It also boils down to being constantly tired and frustrated by the fact that despite the long hours things do not seem to improve much. Everything in this scenario centers on work. The rest of life has been put on indefinite hold.

Because the work related rewards are just about all that is received for sacrificing a majority of one's awake hours, they become the only thing people can use to prove they are succeeding. In their desperation to gain these rewards and to prove that, despite the doubts that keep oozing up, they *are* succeeding, individuals do whatever is necessary. Employees become increasingly self-centered in an effort to maintain self-respect. They become increasingly egotistical.

Is such behavior unethical? I do not think so. When an animal is trapped, it will usually do anything to survive. A great number of people are trapped in their jobs. A great many are struggling for spiritual survival.

Are companies that demand such hours unethical? This is the more difficult question. But, again, I do not think so. Rather, *such companies lack understanding, and understanding in the realm of ethics has to be built on a foundational standard.*

The standard offered by this book is the *development ethic*. If this standard is accepted, *time* itself becomes a key input necessary to the pursuit of all other inputs. Society is responsible for helping individuals find the time required to pursue *all* developmental inputs in a balanced manner. Individuals, in turn, are responsible for supporting society's efforts.

Does a more development-oriented alternative exist in terms of freeing up time? You bet it does. In progressive European countries, for example, the average work week consumes thirty to thirty-five hours as opposed to fifty or sixty in the United States. Also, most European workers are allowed at least six weeks of paid vacation per year, which they take. When everything is added up *it can be estimated that people in the United States work eight weeks or approximately two months more each year than Europeans.*

At the same time, European employees earn more than their counterparts in the United States. To help make this possible, top-level executives do not or are not allowed to reward themselves outlandish compensation packages. In some Western European countries, in fact, a legally defined ratio exists between the compensation available for the lowest- and highest-paid employees—eleven to one, for example, or fifteen to one. Such a ratio obviously encourages the team approach. Top executives can make as much as they want. But to earn a salary increase, top executives must ensure that everyone else in the company, at the same time, receives a raise.

The European perspective comes from social maturity and from an understanding that the development ethic rather than the growth-at-any-cost ethic is the appropriate driving force for societal evolution. Quite simply, in terms of employment most Europeans *work to live rather than living to work.* Life in these countries does not center on the job. A job provides the developmental input of money. But time away from the job is more important to most Europeans than how much more money they can accumulate by sacrificing additional hours or, more to the point, how much more money they can accumulate by *being forced* to work additional hours.

So why isn't the United States moving in this direction as well, why is the work week growing steadily longer instead of shorter? Why, as a culture, are priorities concerning both individual and collective time not shifting? What is blocking change?

A lot of the answer has to do with the way key organization processes are designed, with the way organization management systems are designed. A lot of the answer has to do with the predominance of egoism as the driving force in management circles. A lot of the answer has to do with the competitive/conflict culture spawned by these designs, and by egoism. One important result of such *in-house* competition, which is far less productive than the competition *between* companies and which, according to management guru Peter Drucker, is also far less ethical; one very serious result from a systems perspective is that a lot of time gets wasted, forcing employees to work longer hours.

A lot of time gets wasted, that is, for those who stay employed. It is now necessary to discuss what *else* happens when egoism gets confused with *laissez-faire* economic philosophy. Two of the most counterproductive manifestations of this confusion will be addressed. The first and perhaps the most destructive in terms of our standard is the still popular practice of *downsizing*.

Chapter **10**

When Downsizing Is Unethical

THE DOWNWARD SPIRAL

Downsizing in a majority of instances does not produce positive long-term results. Yet, this vehicle for improving the bottom line was very popular all through the nineties and is still used. On paper, downsizing looks good. But on paper, the calculations are done quantitatively and many of the negative changes that occur during workforce reductions and the ensuing reorganization cannot be quantified.

The reasons corporations give for downsizing include their desire to:

- Combine the responsibilities of two positions into one or eliminate a position, splitting the responsibilities amongst others.
- Eliminate functions seen as not contributing enough to the bottom line.
- Decrease the number of management layers in order to improve communication and to speed up the decision-making process.
- Eliminate duplication of responsibility.
- Get rid of bureaucratic slowdown and reduce overhead by outsourcing traditional staff responsibilities.

Downsizing is expected to enhance productivity and to cut costs, two avenues to improving the bottom line. It must be understood, however, that these two avenues are often at odds. The gains garnered by choosing one can sometimes be offset by resultant losses in the other. Production improvement efforts *do* usually include cost-cutting measures. They can also, however, necessitate additional expense. Cost-cutting efforts, in turn, can improve productivity. Too frequently, however, they instead have an extremely detrimental effect on productivity, especially when downsizing is used.

Despite this, experts are predicting that during the next decade downsizing will remain a primary choice for U.S. companies interested in improving their bottom line. Three *non-cynical* possibilities can be given for continuation of this trend:

1. Corporate heads are not paying attention to the hard lessons learned by peers.

2. Leadership believes that downsizing just hasn't been done correctly and they can devise a successful approach.
3. Due to a lack of appropriate education or training downsizing is the most appealing, or perhaps the only alternative managers can think of when trying to improve the bottom line.

HOW IT'S DONE

One of two approaches is generally used to downsize. The first is early retirement. Older employees are targeted because they usually draw larger salaries. The rationalization sometimes offered to justify this maneuver, although little data exists to support it, is that due to their age, such employees have less energy and are less productive. Financial incentives can be involved. Corporations are frequently surprised, however, by the large number of workers who try to take advantage of an early retirement offer. The problem becomes one of overkill. Too much valuable experience is lost in too many areas. Although savings are realized when slots are not refilled, and from the differential between the salaries of retirees and those of replacement workers, this approach can end up bearing a high price tag.

The second method is to fire employees. This method is less expensive and more controllable because the number of departures is preset. This method is, therefore, more popular. Employees with the largest salaries might be fired first. Or department heads might be ordered to cut their staff by a fixed percentage, say thirty percent. Or an efficiency study might be run to determine who leaves and who stays.

No matter what approach a company adopts, emphasis is on speed. Discuss the plan prior to implementation with as few managers as possible. Encourage them not to leak it. Then, when the downsizing is announced, move those departing out the door as rapidly as possible to prevent damaging the morale of remaining employees. This also allows the company to immediately start rebuilding.

SYSTEMATIC RESULTS OF DOWNSIZING

I recently asked a class of twenty-seven MBA students, all currently holding mid-level management positions, to define the effects of downsizing on key organization systems. Eighteen of these students had personally been through a downsizing. Of the remaining nine, four named a close friend who had experienced downsizing.

Concerning *access to information*, the students agreed that when a downsizing occurs, employees begin hoarding information in order to increase their value. Both intra- and interdepartmental contacts dissolve. After a downsizing, employees frequently have difficulty finding required information because the responsibility for it has been shifted. Those given control over additional files cannot gain access to them. Once access is given, they have trouble determining responsibility for the information in these files.

The students also agreed that employees have less trust in information received following a downsizing. Messages from top-level management are automatically suspect. Information gained from other areas of the organization is also viewed as questionable; reports and numbers have probably been altered to make those writing and tabulating them look more impressive.

Concerning *communication*, the key word is again mistrust. Much of what is heard is considered a smoke screen. Top-down memos are especially suspected. The rumor mill dominates. Everyone looks for hidden meaning in everything they are told.

Concerning *work design*, there is an immediate and heavy work overload for everybody. One reason for this overload is the confusion caused by people suddenly having to take on additional responsibilities without proper training. This confusion causes inefficiencies throughout the organization, because employees too frequently have to learn through trial and error.

Concerning *decision-making and problem-solving*, the students said that emphasis following a downsizing shifts to elimination of risk. Decisions are not as likely to be based on employees' best judgment. Rather, decisions are designed to please bosses. The quality of work usually deteriorates because employees frequently lack the necessary experience or training, and because a sincere effort now seems pointless due to their impression that the company believes everybody expendable. Problem-solving results are less accurate because of the difficulty in gaining access to necessary information. A lack of integration also exists because of the communication breakdown. Units tend to draw protectively inward and to focus on solving their own problems, ignoring the negative effects their solutions might have on other units. The buck is passed whenever possible.

Concerning *rewards*, while the workload and number of work hours required increases, pay often stays the same or decreases following a downsizing. The students disagreed with top-level management's rationalization that the survivors, because they still have jobs, do not mind pay cuts. The students said this added slap in the face heightens already strong feelings of resentment toward bosses. The major reward, job security, is gone. Employees no longer feel in control of their lives. Any promises by upper-level management of better days to come are viewed skeptically. People able to look for jobs with other companies frequently do so, adding to the drain on expertise.

Concerning *discipline*, due to strained relations between management and employees, and to the resultant uneasiness felt by managers, discipline following a downsizing either becomes more severe or disappears totally. Some managers use the insinuation that "You could be next" to control and drive employees. Others tolerate performance shortcomings that should not be tolerated in their efforts to regain employee trust. A "law of the jungle" attitude prevails. Both managers and employees do whatever they must to survive.

Finally, concerning *training and job-related development*, while responsibilities increase following a downsizing, there is less training. One reason offered by personnel managers is that due to the secrecy and rushed atmosphere involved they are not given enough time to plan and implement downsizing-related activities. Another reason is that due to the increased workload, employees have less time for training. A third reason is that training departments often suffer staff reductions during a downsizing.

The employee's perspective concerning training and job-related development also changes. The chief purpose of training frequently shifts to gaining the skills necessary to find a job elsewhere. In terms of career development, employees opt for safe, non-controversial challenges, rather than opportunities that might allow them to gain new knowledge.

IS THERE AN ALTERNATIVE?

Can these reactions be avoided or softened with better preparation? The students thought not. As one class member put it, *"When someone fires shots into a crowd and the bullets whiz by you and hit others instead, the fact that the gunner has forewarned you or apologizes afterward and promises not to fire again does not mean much."*

Most of the literature agrees that the passage of time is the only cure for a slump in post-downsizing morale and productivity. Another factor that helps is a change in upper-level management. Employees hope the new leaders will have different agendas and that job security for workers will be one of their priorities. A third useful approach is the implementation of an intensive training effort to show employees that the company is serious in its commitment to improved performance.

Time, however, is the key ingredient for reviving morale and productivity, and we are talking about *years* rather than months in most cases. Unfortunately, while the bottom line initially improves after a downsizing, such improvements tend to taper off. Attempts to *increase productivity* are hampered by a lack of employee commitment, so that top-level management is forced back into the *cost-cutting* mode. The most convenient vehicle at its disposal for cost cutting is a second round of downsizing. However, there are now fewer resources to juggle. Also, awareness is developing that the company might be permanently alienating its work force.

A question that needs to be addressed at this point is, *"Despite their knowledge concerning the pitfalls of downsizing why do top-level executives persist?"*

Of the three reasons given earlier—lack of attention to other's experiences, a belief that they can do it better, and the perceived lack of an acceptable alternative—the last seems the most plausible. A majority of CEOs are more comfortable with quantitative solutions to corporate problems than with solutions that take into account emotional issues. Downsizing is a quantitative approach to improving the bottom line. Also, few CEOs have received the training necessary to successfully generate employee-driven productivity improvement efforts. They have not received this training on the job because a majority have been locked into their areas of expertise most of the way up the career ladder. They may have attended corporate-sponsored seminars and workshops on the subject; they may have developed some of the understanding and skills required, but not nearly enough to be effective. Those with MBAs have not received the requisite education either, because despite loud protests from a growing number of critics, emphasis in most MBA programs remains on improving specialized skills such as marketing, production, human resources, finance, and accounting. Inadequate attention has been paid to the problem of making employees more productive as individuals, as work units, and as part of a well-integrated, corporate-wide socio-technical system.

This leads to a fourth reason for the continuation of the downsizing trend, one that could be considered *cynical*. This reason also has to do with the quantitative perspective found in most companies.

THE NATURE OF THE BEAST

Companies in the United States continue to focus almost entirely on generating greater amounts of individual wealth. Because the wealth sought so avidly is measured quantitatively and because this is the *only* way to measure it, our quantitative emphasis seeps, consciously or unconsciously, into other important decisions as well. One of the most important of these decisions is how we define employees. Even though employees are different from the widgets they manufacture or the services they deliver, even though they are obviously different from the technology used, even though employees as *purposeful systems* differ from all other items taken into account when calculating ways to improve the bottom line, the tendency is to quantify them as well.

Once quantified, the nature of employees changes. It is no longer necessary to take needs and desires into consideration. With the flick of a pen, a worker can be erased with no feeling of guilt whatsoever because that person is now just part of the scheme of numbers. Downsizing is about cost cutting and costs, at least those taken into account, are defined in terms of numbers.

Sometimes business deteriorates to the point where downsizing is the best path or even the only path to follow. But while those making the decision may be forced to lay employees off when a company is stumbling into bankrupcy, when a recession hits, or when a major share of the market is being taken away by the competition, some executives downsize even when companies are doing well, when sales are increasing, and when the bottom line is improving.

One might wonder why these executives aren't hiring instead of firing? The answer is that they are firing and not hiring because their desire is to improve efficiencies even more. They remain unsatisfied and are willing to sacrifice employees in order to further improve the value of the company's stock. The fact that by sacrificing employees, the decision-makers are probably disrupting the systemic arrangement that makes profit possible in the first place is apparently not an important consideration. The focus is totally on improving short-term value by manipulating the numbers.

Why would those at the top act in such a manner? What motivates them? The reason most frequently offered is that they are simply demonstrating allegiance to the tenets of *laissez-faire economic theory*. But this is not accurate. Once the data starts coming in, once society begins to realize that while the bottom line might improve for a month or two after an unnecessary downsizing the situation in a majority of cases deteriorates rapidly, once this knowledge is in hand, if the driving force behind downsizing is truly *laissez-faire* economic theory, upper-level management would quickly realize that the benefits of downsizing are short-lived and would begin looking for another vehicle to better satisfy its interests.

But upper-level management has not begun looking for another vehicle. Instead, it sticks with downsizing, which means that short-term profit is, indeed, the goal. And, again, why are these people willing to risk so much for the possibility of an immediate improvement in the bottom line?

THE SCARCITY MENTALITY STRIKES AGAIN

In order to answer this question, it is necessary to explore briefly the history of executive compensation. Not too long ago, CEOs and others at the top received salaries set by the corporation's board of directors. Top-level executives in the United States received higher salaries than anywhere else in the world, much higher, frequently by a factor of several hundred percent. And, usually, these salaries were tied in no way to the company's productivity or to its profitability. Even during hard times when profits were dropping or when employees were being laid off, salary levels on the executive levels continued to rise. An example of this phenomenon was the 75-million-dollar salary that Steven J. Ross, chairman of Time Warner Inc., took home while laying off over 600 employees because the communications/magazine industry was not doing very well that year.

Obviously, nobody needs to be paid 75 million dollars. It was a case of blatant egoism with no apologies offered. Such compensation packages were, in fact, part of a competition. People at that level were competing with each other, the objective being to earn more than other CEOs. One of the characteristics of the contest was a total lack of accountability—to stockholders, to customers, to lower-level employees. These people had created their own little world, where only the chosen were allowed to play. The situation was out of control.

A way had to be found to rein them in, to make these people account-able. The solution was to tie the compensation of top-tier executives to the company's bottom line. This was done by making stock options a large part of their package. In order for them to do well, their company had to be doing well, or at least the value of the company's stock had to be increasing, which traditionally occurs when the fortunes of the company are improving.

Problem solved.

Well, not really, for this move, in fact, created an even larger problem. *Employees, rather than simply being ignored by top-level executives, now became a target.* The stock option arrangement benefits executive management only if the value of the company's stock goes up. This happens, as has been said, when the company becomes more profitable. There are two ways to improve a company's profits. The first is to make better use of employee expertise and to encourage employees to design ways to improve productivity. The second way involves bringing efficiency experts in to cut costs. While the first way is more effective in the long run, it takes more time. The second way, especially if it results in downsizing, produces quicker results. When employees are laid off, bottom-line improvement can occur, literally, overnight. Thus, executives first began looking for "dead wood" to get rid of. Then they began looking for wood not quite dead but expendable in that the operation could probably survive without it.

Another false manifestation of the link between *laissez-faire* economic theory and egoism that made good use of downsizing was the *takeover* movement that peaked during the nineties. The men who led this movement would gain controlling interest in companies, cut the workforce, make those who remained labor harder for the same or less pay, sell off whatever assets they could, and then either let the company fall apart or sell the shell. The *only* concern in such situations was the amount of personal profit that could be squeezed out. Nothing else and nobody else mattered.

In both cases, the rationalization was that downsizing increased the efficiency of the operation, and that stockholders and society in general benefited. In reality, while some shareholders benefited, society usually did not. Most certainly company employees suffered, both those laid off and those spared. According to "Few Recover Totally from Downsizing," an arti-cle that appeared in the August 1998 edition of *U.S. Today*, the majority of workers laid off during a downsizing, when they can find another job, earn just eighty-five percent of what they would have earned if they had stayed in their original job. Those over fifty earn on average just sixty-five percent of their previous salaries.

Although our gross national product (GNP) has been steadily improv-ing and executive compensation packages have gone through the roof, "The Downsizing of America," a *New York Times* special report published in 1998, explains that after adjusting for inflation the 1996 median wage was nearly three percent lower than what it was in 1979, and that while the *average* household income climbed ten percent during this same period, ninety-five percent of the growth was enjoyed by the wealthiest twenty percent of the population.

ETHICAL AND SYSTEMIC IMPLICATIONS

Downsizing, in most instances, is an exercise in raw egoism. *Laissez-faire* economics is used as an excuse, but egoism is the driving force. Increasingly, the media is bringing to light the hypocrisy of those who continue to use this vehicle to enhance their own wealth, showing the extent of this hypocrisy from a bottom line as well as a societal perspective. Even the *Wall Street Journal*, a bastion of *laissez-faire* economic thought that initially lauded downsizing as appropriate and necessary to maintaining the health of our corporations and of our economy, now periodically publishes pieces denouncing the motives, the shortsightedness, and the egoism of those practicing it.

When one looks at downsizing from the perspective of ethics, the results are usually negative. Downsizing satisfies utilitarian criteria only for those still advocating the economic man theory generated during the early Industrial Revolution, only for those who still believe that the sole pursuit important to improvement of the human condition is the pursuit of increased wealth. Of course, the economic man theory didn't work then, and it doesn't work now. One might suspect, based on the lessons of history, that it will never work, no matter what the economic conditions are.

Concerning the deontological approach to ethics, the only law being followed during a downsizing is the *law of the jungle*. Regarding relativism, downsizing is an example of the dark side of this school, where consensus is never really sought, where a small group forces its decision, its will on the majority. Rather than a union between *laissez-faire economic theory* and *egoism*, therefore, what emerges in the case of unnecessary downsizing is a union between *egoism* and *relativism* driven by people who have never stopped competing, by people who suffer from *adolescent arrest*, people who will do whatever is necessary to win.

Concerning the universal ethical standard being offered, downsizing, of course, is about as detrimental as it gets. As was said earlier, there are times when workforce reduction is the only hope left. It becomes necessary for the organization to survive. *But the decision to downsize should occur only after all else has been tried, only after everyone in the company has brought their ideas and expertise to bear on finding ways to increase efficiencies and to improve productivity.*

When this is done the organization has remained true to the universal standard. But when in order to improve the bottom line companies make downsizing their first choice, when they focus on erasing numbers, they are behaving unethically. They are not giving their most powerful resource a chance. They are acting egotistically, hoarding decision-making authority, and denying the rest of the workforce the opportunity to assist. They are doing so, of course, to protect their own short-term interests.

At the same time, when such unnecessary downsizing occurs, as has been shown, the systemic nature of the operation is destroyed. Rather than a well-integrated whole the organization breaks down into an aggregate of pieces, each unit, each individual following the example of the leaders, looking out for itself, for himself with no further concern for the interactions necessary to a smooth and profitable operation.

DOING THE RIGHT THING

As an alternative to downsizing, progressive U.S. corporate leaders, along with their European and Asian counterparts, are beginning to realize that increased profitability can also be achieved by involving employees more fully in the improvement of products, manufacturing processes, management systems, and the work environment. Instead of getting rid of employees, the objective is to better utilize their expertise. Progressive CEOs understand that if organized properly, this approach starts producing positive bottom-line results almost immediately, and that these results, rather than tapering off, snowball.

How is the required level of participation orchestrated? One excellent vehicle is a quality-improvement effort. A systemic approach to quality improvement is built around an organization-wide network of teams, an adequate set of process ground rules agreed to by everyone, an ongoing familarization process, technical and management systems training, the introduction of statistical measurement techniques when applicable, and an ongoing long- and short-term planning exercise. When all these pieces are in place and properly integrated, the CEO usually has to worry about problems of expansion, rather than about layoffs.

In summary, then, downsizing has proven to be a short-term, short-sighted approach to improving the bottom line. There is no way to implement downsizing without adversely affecting employee morale and creating confusion in key management systems. Immediate savings are quickly offset by long-term systemic problems.

Powerful foreign competitors understand this. Too many corporate leaders in the United States, however, do not understand, or do not care. For those who *do* care, in order to deal with the problem, in order to change attitudes and encourage exploration of more effective alternatives, it is time to rethink the traditional approach to *training*, whether it be delivered on-site by staff and consultants or in the university classroom. Such training should focus *less* on the enhancement of quantitative and technical skills and *more* on developing management's ability to increase the contribution of employees as cost-cutters, innovators, and quality enhancers.

Before a new approach to training can be designed, however, it is necessary to deal with the second counterproductive manifestation of the marriage between the *laissez-faire* economic philosophy and egoism. This is the traditional evaluation and reward system. Evaluation and reward, according to systems theory, is the cornerstone of company culture. The effectiveness of training, along with the effectiveness of every other organization process, depends on the behaviors reinforced by evaluation and reward. If the wish is to modify an organization's culture, if the wish is to improve the results of training or of problem-solving efforts or of production efforts, if a more effective alternative to downsizing is sought, the first thing that must be addressed is the way employees are evaluated and rewarded.

Chapter 11

Evaluation and Reward: The Primary Shapers of Culture

KEY ORGANIZATION PROCESSES AS THE WELLSPRING

The second counterproductive manifestation of the union between *laissez-faire* economic theory and the egoism school of ethical thought in the modern-day workplace is the traditional evaluation and reward process. It does not, however, stand alone in this respect. *The way a majority of company processes have historically been designed contributes as much to the disempowerment as it does to the empowerment of employees.* These processes, including communication, access to information, decision-making, work design, training, and evaluation and reward are the glue that binds company functions together. How they do so is critical to shaping the culture and the ethical climate of the organization. Before focusing on evaluation and reward, therefore, it might be of value to discuss briefly the strengths and weaknesses of the other processes.

Communication **is first.** When people seek access or feedback and continually run into barriers created by a competitive environment, they either begin looking for ways around the barriers, or they quit and proceed without the contact. In both cases, time is wasted. Allowing people to talk directly with anyone they wish, without messages having to work their way up and down the hierarchy, keeps content from being distorted or from being changed purposely. Open communication also helps clarify responsibility for what is being said.

Access to information **is second.** When a company organizes its information dissemination processes in a way that guarantees all employees easy access, it increases the effectiveness of the operation. In terms of ethics, an approach that ensures such access keeps people from hoarding information to gain job security or increase power. Open access to information prevents companies from taking advantage of their employees. It allows employees to utilize their potential more fully, which reduces frustration, improves morale, and improves the ethical climate as well as the bottom line.

Decision-making **is third.** The participation of employees in shaping decisions that affect them gains commitment to those decisions. It improves chances for implementation. The employees now *own* the decisions, want to see them succeed, and will work to keep others from blocking them. If the decision turns out to be wrong, scapegoating is no longer an option, as everybody has contributed. Finally, this approach prevents the unethical behavior that occurs when an individual or a small group of people make decisions in isolation.

The argument for involving employees in the **design of their work** as a means of avoiding unethical behavior follows much the same logic. The design becomes *their* design. They understand it. They want to show that it is effective. If they run into problems with the initial design, employees now have the power to change it.

Training **is fourth.** Training is one of the most poorly worked out concepts in the modern-day workplace. The problem is with the difference between "teaching" and "learning" discussed in Chapter 1. Too frequently, sessions are largely a waste of employee time, not delivering much that is useful or not delivering the material in an effective manner. Sitting through a canned training session can be extremely frustrating. More discussion on training will be included later.

All of the above processes affect the ethical climate in an organization either directly or indirectly. All are important. The process that does the most to shape that climate, however, the one that has the most impact on ethics is the **evaluation and reward** process. The rewards received for work done serve as the bottom line for employees. Evaluation helps shape the size of that bottom line. The issue addressed in this chapter is that most organization evaluation and reward processes encourage *egoism* rather than *utilitarianism*, or even *enlightened egoism*. They encourage individual employees to focus entirely on themselves and to treat their peers as the enemy. By doing so, they thwart the development of their own and others' potential.

WHY THE TRADITIONAL APPROACH TO EVALUATION AND REWARD IS UNETHICAL

A traditional performance appraisal system works like this. At the beginning of the year, the manager and employee sit down together to define the employee's goals for that year based on department and organization objectives. Theoretically, this gives the employee direction and incentive while providing the manager with means to measure the employee's contribution. During this process, the manager and employee focus on two criteria. The first criteria is actual results the employee is responsible for (reports, projects, production numbers). The second is the way the employee works (communication skills, decisiveness, commitment, industriousness, the ability to function as a team member).

At the end of the year, the manager and employee sit down again and discuss why the employee has exceeded, met, or fallen short of expectations. The manager then writes an evaluation. The employee signs this evaluation and has the opportunity to submit a rebuttal. The document then goes into the employee's file and theoretically plays a role in determining raises and promotions.

This approach contains a number of weaknesses. First, due to the ever increasing rate of change in markets, in technology, and in social trends this year's goals might be obsolete within months or weeks. At that point the employee has two choices. The first is to forge on without altering the appraisal and to attempt at year's end to explain what has happened. The second is to sit down with the manager and to revise initial goals. The problem with the second choice is again one of *time*, especially when the already overloaded manager might have to do this with a number of direct reports.

In addition, most managers, due to other demands, cannot pay adequate attention to individual employee performance during the course of the year. This results in an evaluation based more so on impressions than on actual, ongoing observations, which, in turn, leads employees to play political games, vying for a high level of visibility with the manager, focusing on making the right impression rather than on getting their job done.

Performance evaluations also frequently inhibit creativity and the willingness to deal with systemic problems. Employees do not want to extend themselves, to define new challenges, or to suggest something out of the ordinary. They want to play it safe. They want to make sure they can reach the goals agreed upon. At the same time, once employees do set out to meet their goals, they tend to work around weaknesses encountered in organization systems instead of stopping to fix them. Such repair efforts do not appear on their list of required activities and, therefore, have no value, at least no direct value to the individual's career. Employees view such weaknesses in organization systems as obstacles to success, rather than as improvements necessary to the company's long-term health. They view them as stumbling blocks to be avoided.

A fourth problem also has to do with defining *individual* work-related goals. This approach usually runs contrary to the cooperative team approach important to meeting the ethical standard proposed. Such a requirement forces employees to focus entirely on their own fortunes, sometimes to the detriment of co-workers.

The performance appraisal was created to facilitate the free-enterprise system. Advocates of the appraisal system believe that those who work the hardest and most effectively, those who contribute the most, should benefit the most financially and in terms of advancement. The evaluation process defines the level of individual employee contribution so that the reward level can be set to match it.

Unfortunately, practice in the modern workplace rarely follows philosophy. As is obvious from the discussion in Chapter 10, top-level management's reward is rarely tied to productivity. While productivity and profits are going down, the CEO's reward is frequently still going up. At the same time, relating performance directly to productivity down in the trenches is becoming increasingly difficult. More and more of the workforce is involved in generating and disseminating information, in providing services rather than in the direct production of widgets that can be counted.

Even when managers can measure productivity, it doesn't usually make much difference. Raises at this point in the evolution of management and financial theory normally are based more on departmental budget restrictions than on individual contributions. The manager's main concern in most cases is how to allocate salary increases in a way that will upset the smallest number of people, rather than how to define who has contributed the most.

In terms of promotions, the chances of getting one usually depend largely on who upstairs likes the employee. That, in turn, frequently depends as much on personality as it does on performance. Subjectivity, competition, and politics again play major roles in the exercise. Employees know this. Some take advantage of it. Most resent it. In either case, the organization's overall ethical climate, especially when viewed from the perspective of our standard, cannot help but be negatively affected.

All companies want to continually improve their performance. They want to improve their products, their manufacturing or service delivery processes, their management systems, and their work environment. The major requirement for such efforts is, or should be, to take full advantage of employee expertise on all levels and to integrate that expertise in the most effective manner. To meet this requirement we need three interdependent things. First, we need a cooperative rather than a conflict-ridden culture, we need a culture where employees expend their energies supporting rather than trying to beat each other. Second, we need an integrated team approach. Third, we need an organization-wide, holistic perspective.

The traditional performance evaluation is antithetical to all three of these requirements. One of the characteristics usually measured during the process is the ability to work with others. But the typical reward system into which the evaluation feeds allows only a small percentage of employees to receive the top-level pay increase and gives only one employee the promotion based on compared performances. This situation automatically pits workers against each other, the question becoming, "How can I appear to be working with and supporting my in-house competitors while at the same time making sure they don't get ahead?" Such mental calculations and the resultant machinations invariably create a schizoid, highly stressful environment.

Concerning teamwork, when rewards are individualized what happens should be quite obvious. Mary and Peter are on the same team. Mary gets credit for being a good team player and is rewarded. Peter is not. Peter can do two things. He can quit the team and spend his time sulking and telling people why the team approach doesn't really work, or he can begin competing against Mary, seeing if he can become the better team player, while at the same time making her look not quite so good. *What we end up with in this scenario are people competing to see who can be the most cooperative, if that makes any sense.*

The kind of interaction too frequently created by individualizing evaluations and rewards in the workplace resembles that found on a professional basketball team where players' salaries are tied to the number of points they score in each game. The effect of such a strategy on team performance is immediately obvious to sports fans. Why, then, is it not obvious to corporate executives?

AND TO MAKE MATTERS WORSE

Forcing employees to focus on their individual performance as opposed to the performance of their team, department, or organization as a whole is dangerous in another way. The fact that an individual excels does not necessarily mean that the organization as a whole does well. In fact, when the focus is totally on oneself and when the focus is totally egotistical, the organization as a whole rarely does well. To make matters worse, companies have, for all the wrong reasons, been using the *bell-shaped density curve* (BSDC) to shape decisions concerning salary and raises.

The BSDC is a statistical concept developed to describe the distribution of data points when discussing one characteristic of a population. It has been sorely misused in the business world and is a major obstruction in efforts to improve ethics. For decades, the BSDC has been used as a frame of reference for defining workforce performance. While the intention has been to improve productivity, a major result, unavoidably, has been to limit the amount of improvement possible and to sew seeds of discontent.

This is a pretty strong statement. Before elaborating, it is necessary to describe in detail exactly what the BSDC is. According to popular belief this statistical tool says that when a characteristic varies in a population it generally follows the same pattern. Most data points are similar and lie in the middle of the range. A smaller number lie at one end, a smaller number lie at the other end. Thus, for example, most people stand between the heights of 5'6" and 5'10"; a smaller number taper off at heights above 5'10"; a smaller number taper off at heights beneath 5'6". In the world of work we have decided that most employees produce an average amount. A smaller number produce an above-average amount. A smaller number produce a below-average amount. Where an employee fits into this scheme allows us to determine what the size of her raise should be.

The involved logic is simple, maybe even useful in terms of easing the decision-making process. *But it is wrong.*

There are several serious faults with using the BSDC to determine raises, faults that ultimately keep organizations from more fully realizing their potential. Probably the most serious fault is that the concept has never been proven valid. It is not a law, not even a theory. It is a statistics-based descriptive device that demonstrates a curve population characteristic data points *sometimes* follow. It is a phenomenon interesting to scientists but it is *not* one of science's building blocks.

The BSDC was first defined in 1733 by a man named DeMoivre, then redefined a half-century later by two astronomers named LaPlace and Gauss, who used it to describe the behavior of errors in astronomical measurements. The curve shows up significantly only in large populations—natural, mechanical, or human. When we say *large* we are talking about thousands or hundreds of thousands of data points, even millions. The smaller the sample size, as scientists know, the less chance of the curve accurately portraying the true distribution of the characteristic being defined.

This fault has two parts. First, the BSDC is not a given. Forcing population characteristics to fit it, therefore, is invalid scientifically and, in the workplace situation, wrong ethically once we understand the error of our thinking. Second, even if the population as a whole (all employees in the United States lumped together, for example) *does* fit the curve in terms of productivity, using it to define the productivity of smaller units (offices, departments, divisions, individual companies) is invalid scientifically, and in the workplace situation, wrong, ethically once we understand the error of our thinking.

Does a more systemic or a more ethical alternative to employee evaluation exist? Do we have an alternative that comes closer to satisfying the standard? One company that got beyond the myth of the BSDC was a Philadelphia area paper distributorship started in 1990. Because the CEO, Doug, was progressive he decided to involve all of his employees in the design of key processes. When representatives from the different departments met, the first thing they wanted to address was compensation. Such companies traditionally have two sales forces, outside and inside. Outside salespeople make the initial contacts, develop face-to-face relationships, and are paid through commissions. Inside salespeople, who handle the details, are salaried.

The inside salespeople at Doug's company said they didn't think this arrangement was fair as they were just as important to the success of the transaction as the outside people. The inside salespeople wanted part of the commission. Next the secretaries, warehouse people, and drivers said their services were also important to the success of the sale and that they too should receive a share of the commission.

The result of these conversations was a three-tiered financial compensation system. Everyone received minimal salaries. Raises were based on longevity rather than on performance. A team was built around each outside salesperson and his territory. A percentage of the profits generated by each team was divided among all team members. This arrangement obviously encouraged cooperation. A larger percentage of these profits, however, was put into a company pool to be split among all company employees. This was done to encourage cooperation between teams as well as cooperation between the members of individual teams.

The next issue addressed was the evaluation process. With such a compensation system in place, how could management effectively evaluate performance? The group went through all the traditional approaches—managers evaluating their reports, reports evaluating their managers, managers and reports evaluating each other, employees evaluating themselves, peers evaluating each other, everybody evaluating everybody they interacted with. None of these approaches seemed to fit.

It eventually became clear that they didn't fit because, in this situation, the traditional approach to employee evaluation didn't make sense. The employees of this company now had real incentive to work together. If a team member was having a problem, who would gain the most from stepping in immediately to help? When it came to hiring new team members, who stood to gain the most from hiring the most qualified candidate? Finally, who should be in charge of terminating employees who, despite the assistance offered, eventually proved themselves incapable of doing their job? Who best understood an employee's shortcomings and would gain the most from replacing that person?

Evaluation in this company became a participative, integrated, ongoing part of work. Everyone was evaluating everyone, but on an informal, continuous basis. The objective in this instance was to make everyone a winner, to produce teams full of winners, to produce a company full of winners.

THE NORM

This approach to evaluation and reward, obviously, makes extremely good sense. How, then, does our case study vary from the norm? This is where the myth of the BSDC comes in. The BSDC played no role in the design of the reward and evaluation systems at the paper distributorship.

Yet, in too many companies today it lies at the heart of these systems, thus thwarting improvement.

When modern-day companies talk about change, they frequently mean fine-tuning their current culture, making it increasingly efficient, eventually to the point of maximum return. The current quality improvement effort is a good example of this perspective. But these companies quickly begin to spin their wheels because productivity doesn't reach the desired level and they don't know what to do next. Frustration replaces early feelings of achievement. The companies find themselves trapped in a "dilemma," which means they find themselves trapped in a problematic situation that cannot be resolved in its current context.

The context referred to in this situation is the organization's culture. *"Efficiency" enhancing efforts have to do with getting the most from the current culture, rather than with changing it. "Effectiveness" enhancing efforts, on the other hand, have to do with making change in the culture necessary to improved performance in all sectors and on all levels.*

Organizations frequently find change on the *effectiveness* level too intense, too threatening. Most, therefore, never get beyond the increased efficiency orientation. Evidence of increased efficiency is immediate improvement in the bottom line. The bottom line can be improved by getting more out of your employees or by getting rid of them. The BSDC is a vehicle used to help decide which employees to get rid of. This makes it a negative incentive, whereas realization of our standard requires positive incentives.

In summation, the growing number of organizations that are risking effectiveness enhancing efforts realize quickly that the organization's evaluation and reward system more than any other shapes culture and affects the organization's ability to change. The evaluation and reward system, therefore, must be a primary target for redesign if increased effectiveness is the goal.

In order to justify what has just been said, it is necessary to discuss how positive cultural change occurs. It can occur, basically, in two ways. First, the boss can mandate it. ("We will start doing things differently or heads will roll.") Second, all those affected can participate in the redesign effort, and in implementation of the new design. Most modern-day organization change efforts are a combination of the two ways listed above. However, emphasis remains too frequently on the first way, when it should be on the second.

Any change effort has three stages—design, implementation, and feedback and further modification. In boss-driven efforts, the design stage usually progresses relatively rapidly. It is much easier for one person to make all the decisions than to integrate the ideas of a large number of employees. It is during the implementation stage, however, that the participatory approach catches up and pulls away. When employees have contributed to a design improvement, they understand it. They have gained ownership, as has been said, and will strive to make implementation successful. When it is the boss's idea, employees tend to leave it up to the boss, or to do exactly what they are told without question, even when they see problems looming.

In terms of the feedback and further modification stage, it is a lot easier to discover weaknesses and to make improvements in a participative project than in one that is some boss's pet project.

NEED FOR A COOPERATIVE ENVIRONMENT

The point is that the cultural change being talked about occurs most easily in a cooperative environment, in an environment where employees want to work together, to share knowledge and ideas, and to trust each other. The way that the evaluation and reward systems is designed decides whether an organization's culture is cooperative or whether conflict in its many disguises prevails.

The traditional design of these systems pits employees against each other. Therefore, *organizations that mount change efforts without addressing the issue of evaluation and rewards as part of the process are sending a schizoid message.* "Yes, we understand the importance of team-driven improvement; we understand the need for a cooperative effort. But when it gets right down to the nitty-gritty, we still expect you to fight it out."

How many people are familiar with companies where the previously mentioned BSDC-based performance evaluation system breaks the workforce down into categories of twenty percent superior, sixty percent average, and twenty percent not up to snuff? How many know of companies where an employee ranked in the lowest twenty percent for two evaluations in a row is in danger of losing her job?

Employees who find themselves on this lowest level are expected to do whatever is necessary to climb out, opening a slot for someone else to fall into. Finally, some companies add insult to injury by declaring, as has previously been said, that "the ability and willingness to work as part of a team" is one of the criteria upon which the performance evaluation is built.

RESPECT AS KEY

Salary and keeping one's job were the original incentives to improved performance. In the modern-day workplace, however, these are no longer the only incentives or even the most important incentives. Once a reasonable level of income is reached the most important modern business world incentive has proven time and again to be *respect*, that management takes the employees' needs and desires into account, that management respects the employees' potential, the employees' ideas, and the employees' individuality.

The companies that have done the best, the Motorolas, the W. L. Gores, the Solectrons, the Harley Davidsons, the Semcos, the Men's Warehouses, the

Wegman's Food Markets, the Johnsonville Sausages, and the L. L. Beans have been, quite simply, those that have shown the most respect for employee potential, that have encouraged employees to contribute as much as possible according to their expertise, that have encouraged employees to work as a team, rewarding them for doing so rather than pitting them against each other.

These companies have understood the very simple fact that management's objective should be to help *every* employee become part of the most productive twenty percent, so that the most productive twenty percent becomes, instead, the most productive one hundred percent. They have understood that insisting on a BSDC to define performance is counterproductive when dealing with a workforce capable of constant improvement. They have understood that the best results are generated when employees are supporting each other's efforts. They have understood that in such situations management *facilitation* rather than management *control* is the key to success.

The next question is, once companies stop downsizing and begin focusing, instead, on more effective utilization of workforce expertise, once companies see the error of their ways and design an evaluation and reward system that provides a positive incentive rather than a negative incentive, that encourages employees to utilize their expertise to help the company not only meet but exceed its objectives, how can the cultural change we have set the stage for be orchestrated?

The key concept here is *empowerment*. The standard introduced in Chapter 6 cannot be used effectively as a vehicle to improved ethics unless companies are willing to empower employees. Empowerment is also *the* key component of the systems approach. But just as many companies may claim to be managing in a systemic manner when, in actuality, they are not, many companies may also claim to have empowered their workforce when, in fact, they have not.

Chapter 12, therefore, will discuss what it takes to empower a workforce effectively.

Chapter 12

To Empower or Not to Empower, That Is the Question

WHAT *IS* EMPOWERMENT?

A dictionary definition of the verb *to empower* is "to permit or enable." From a systemic perspective, these are two very different actions. "To permit" is to allow people to do something they were previously not allowed to do. "To enable" is to provide the resources necessary to the achievement of an objective. Both actions, however, are required when we are talking about systemic empowerment in the workplace or about implementation of our standard. Employees must be "permitted" to realize their potential and to utilize it to make improvements. Also, employees must be "enabled" by providing them with the resources necessary to the realization and utilization of this potential. From a systems perspective, therefore, the definition of the verb *to empower* should include both. It should be "to permit *and* to enable" rather than "to permit *or* to enable."

"Empowerment" has been a buzzword for a long while now. It remains very popular, especially among top-level executives. Despite the ongoing interest, however, most organization efforts to empower the workforce have failed to produce the desired results; they have failed to generate the desired level of employee commitment. The key word in this last sentence, of course, is not *failed*, but *most*. It indicates that there are, indeed, companies that have mounted successful empowerment efforts, companies where the critical pieces are all present, properly aligned, and integrated, companies where bottom-line improvement is long-term and where the level of morale has risen and remains high without endless pep rallies.

If this is true, if such success stories exist (and they do) the rest, one would think, should be easy. We must simply identify the involved companies and figure out how they did it. Then we need only adjust the model to meet the needs of our own operation, and implement it. But that has not happened. It hasn't happened because the managers at all levels in many organizations, while wanting the efforts to succeed, are not prepared to permit the changes in their own culture necessary to success. They want improvement, they understand the need to get employees more fully involved in the decision making process; they understand the need to make better use of employee expertise and potential. But, at the same time, the traditional manager has limits beyond which he is unwilling to go.

The most restricting of these limits is that managers insist on maintaining the degree of control inherent to their position. And this is the rub. The key to the success stories is that *managers in these companies have been willing to give up much of their traditional control in order to truly empower employees.*

Without empowerment, nothing else in an improvement effort bears fruit—not attempts to gain commitment, not enhanced training, not attempts at better integration, not attempts to improve the ethical climate. Empowerment is the key. That is why most companies set on improving their operations and bottom line begin by sending employees to seminars on empowerment, show tapes on empowerment and invite guest speakers to talk about empowerment. Employees are frequently, as has been said, even sent to visit successful efforts mounted by other companies in order to bring ideas back on how best to empower the workforce.

It is not that they do not pay attention. Trainees listen carefully to what they are told at the seminars and take notes. But what they miss, what they fail to carry back in their notebooks (probably because it is too far out of sync with their current reality) is the need to empower the workforce *fully* rather than *partially.*

"Wait just one minute," I hear immediately from the audience. "We empower our employees fully! We train them in team dynamics, we train them in problem-solving techniques and conflict resolution. Then we put them on teams and assign the teams important projects to work on. And when the work is completed, *everybody* who has contributed is thanked, congratulated, and rewarded, not just the managers."

Any organization seriously committed to empowerment truly believes it has made the necessary effort and will defend that effort vigorously. The problem is not one of intent, rather, it is one of degree. Those guiding a majority of current empowerment efforts have confused the concept of *partial empowerment* with that of *full empowerment* and the two are quite different. This shortcoming is serious because, as systems thinkers have long realized, *partial empowerment generates only partial commitment in employees and produces, at best, partial success.*

THE PROBLEM WITH PARTIAL EMPOWERMENT

Perhaps the easiest way to make understandable what has just been said is to use a familiar analogy—child rearing. When offspring reach adolescence, parents no longer want to treat them like children, no longer want simply to tell them what to do and then make sure they do it. Rather, parents want their offspring to begin exercising judgment and to begin making at least some of the decisions. Owing to their kids' lack of experience, however, mom and dad continue to set policy upon which their kids are expected to base decisions. They also reserve the right to overrule. Ultimately, therefore, the parents remain in charge and make sure that their kids understand this, because mom and dad are not quite ready, not quite comfortable enough yet to cut their kids completely loose.

When managers partially empower employees, they are treating the employees like adolescent youngsters rather than like grown-ups. This is a costly mistake. Managers want employee input. They want employees to begin contributing to decisions. But most managers also want to make sure that the employees understand the manager is still in charge. They want employees to understand that the manager still has the final say and will make the final decision.

The problem is that in the workplace most employees are not adolescents, but adults, just like the managers. The problem is that employees function best when treated as adults, not adolescents. As adults, these employees spend the majority of their waking hours solving problems, making decisions, handling family finances, settling disputes, managing projects, and working as equals with others to improve the community. They do all the things normal adults do, take on all the responsibilities normal adults take on.

In too many organizations, however, each time they pass through the office or shop door, employees are forced to regress to adolescence. They are expected to wait until their boss tells them how to resolve problems they would normally have no difficulty solving. They are not allowed to communicate directly with one another, but are required to go through their manager. They are forced to get permission to make common-sense procedural adjustments.

One rationalization given by management for the partial empowerment approach is that it must maintain control in order to effectively integrate the changes being generated. Management has defined the organization's long-range objectives. It best understands them, and, therefore, best understands what should be worked on, when, where, and how. Management has the overview, the necessary model of how things need to fit together in its mind. If lower-level employees begin making changes without access to this information, costly mistakes and unnecessary confusion will result.

The rebuttal to this argument, of course, is that in the systemic, full empowerment approach to organization change, *all* employees are familiar with the company's long-term objectives. The definition of these objectives has been an ongoing, participative part of the process. *All* employees have contributed to their identification and fine-tuning.

So, that is the difference between partial and full empowerment. Positive results are, of course, possible with partial empowerment. That has been proven. But it has also become obvious that positive results take longer to materialize with partial empowerment, that they are frequently not the results companies are looking for (at least in terms of magnitude), and that they frequently leave both the company and employees frustrated.

The full empowerment model, which obviously fits better with our ethical standard, is superior in terms of achieving overall organization objectives. The full empowerment model is also easier to implement and cheaper once the necessary changes are accepted. Nonetheless, management has dug itself into a partial empowerment rut and is stuck. Until management becomes unstuck, until it finds its way out of the rut, until it makes the cultural changes necessary, companies will continue to be frustrated in terms of improving both their bottom line and their ethical climate.

How do companies dig their way out of this partial empowerment rut? A case study will help clarify what is being discussed. It will help demonstrate the subtleness of what has been happening in traditional business settings where those in charge lack the necessary systemic perspective.

OFF TO A BAD START

Most case studies concerning empowerment discuss what the author believes to be a successful effort. In this instance, however, a company shall be discussed that did almost everything wrong. What this company put into place with the best of intentions is quite similar to what most U.S. companies interested in utilizing employee expertise more fully put into place. Its results are quite similar to the results most companies end up with. The company about to be described deals with insurance. It will be called Company X. Passages printed normally from this point on will define the actions taken by Company X in its effort to improve productivity through empowerment. The italicized passages will include explanations from a systems perspective on why most of the involved actions were non-effective at best and counter-productive at worst.

The empowerment effort at Company X that was introduced by the executive board after a reengineering project, complete with the usual downsizing, ended up hurting the bottom line rather than helping it.

Reengineering, a concept originally developed by Henry Ford to improve technical manufacturing processes was reintroduced in recent years as a means of making the workforce, in combination with technology more efficient. Unfortunately, in too many cases, reengineering has become simply another excuse for downsizing. When an empowerment effort is begun in an attempt to clean up the mess after a misguided reengineering or downsizing effort, employees are naturally suspicious of upper-level management's motives. The key ingredient to success—employee commitment—is much harder to generate. If Company X had launched a comprehensive empowerment exercise before reengineering, and had involved the employees on all levels in efforts to improve the operation, greater efficiencies would have been realized in a wider range of areas with fewer negative consequences.

After the employee empowerment process was introduced to top-level management by the board, division vice presidents were given the responsibility of presenting it to their units and getting things started. They were told that their degree of success in doing so would affect their performance evaluation. How the vice presidents organized the effort in their individual units was left up to them.

> Immediately, Company X introduced three elements that are antithetical to a successful empowerment. The first was "top-downism." Top-level management, rather than convincing the division vice presidents that supporting the process would benefit themselves as well as the company said, in effect, "You will get involved! You will empower your reports! We are holding your performance evaluation as a club over your head to make sure that you do." People usually react best to a logical explanation delivered in a respectful manner, especially one that includes a definition of the benefits to themselves. At the same time, people resent being threatened, no matter how subtle the threat, and will resist, the resistance not usually taking the form of open defiance but, rather, disguising itself as part of normal job pressures. An example would be employees in a resisting manager's department suddenly becoming too busy with their normal workload to participate in process related activities.
>
> The second antithetical element introduced was competition. Employee performance evaluations, as has been said, are typically compared in order to decide who gets the raise and who gets the promotion. Vice presidents in Company X immediately found themselves pitted against each other. The competitive environment was intensified by the fact that the way each vice president got things started, the way each of them introduced the effort and shaped it in his individual division was left to that person's discretion. Thus, the vice presidents were encouraged to try to beat each other, rather than to share expertise and to cooperate, when sharing and cooperation are foundational to both the systems approach and to achievement of the ethical standard defined.
>
> The third antithetical element introduced was fragmentation. Two things that bind successful empowerment processes together and that allow the necessary integration of efforts going on all over the organization are a common language and communication. When each unit is doing its own thing, the necessary common language does not exist. Also, because of the competitive environment, communication between units tends to decrease rather than to increase. Even if one division's effort is highly successful, therefore, due to the lack of integrating communication, its effects on the organization as a whole might be negative.

GOING THE INDIVIDUALIZED ROUTE

In at least one area, the claims division, the first step taken was to bring in a consultant to assess employee attitudes and employee perceptions concerning division performance and problems. Focus groups were formed and members surveyed for opinions.

> Two different approaches to empowerment are the individual-oriented approach and the systems-oriented approach. The individual-oriented approach focuses initially on the employee and tries to discover what she is feeling, what and who the employee thinks the problem is, and how the employee thinks the issues should be addressed, usually through a survey. The information gathered from individuals is then consolidated, studied, fed back, and discussed. Eventually, key issues are defined and task forces are formed to deal with them.
>
> The systems approach focuses instead on organization design. It believes that if the planning, communication, access to information, decision making, work design, training, and evaluation and reward systems are made to function more effectively, most of the individual issues will disappear. Rather than first surveying employees to gather information for top-level management and consultants to analyze, the systems approach immediately gives employee teams on all levels the authority to identify, design, and implement process improvements in their own areas of expertise. The individual obviously remains a key player in this scenario but the initial focus is now on the system rather than on the isolated employee.

Also, with the individual approach the survey is, once again, something done to *the employee, orchestrated and controlled by top management. When the systems approach is used and the workforce is given control employees immediately take charge and begin deciding what they want to do and how they should do it.*

The results of this survey were given to division top-level management, which announced that after a thorough review they would be released to the workforce. What happened, in fact, was that only a carefully edited version of survey results, containing what many considered to be severe distortions of what had been said, was fed back to contributors.

So much for empowerment. So much for trust. So much for any serious attempt by the workforce to make improvements. Any commitment to the process that might have been generated up to this point was now dead. Management obviously had its own agenda. From that point on the employees would do and say as little as possible, and only things they thought were expected. In other words, it was back to business as usual, although the employees would have to continue pretending they were involved.

THE ROCK AND THE HARD PLACE

An advisory group was formed to pick three issues out of the pages generated by the survey. These issues were then passed on to a Continuous Improvement Committee (CIC), including representatives from all employee levels, to be worked on. The CIC was charged with forming task forces to study the issues before making recommendations to the Division Lead Team (DLT) composed of the division vice president and upper-level managers. After the DLT had defined the course of action to be followed, the CIC was responsible for communicating and supporting its decisions concerning action steps.

The three issues picked were identifying possible improvements in the division's approach to indemnity and expense management, identifying ways to improve customer service, and identifying ways to enhance employee development. It was made clear by upper-level management that employee development projects were not a priority. Also, the vice president of the claims division said that he wanted quick results from the task forces formed to explore each of the three issues, although their efforts should not interfere with normal work.

This is a mainly top-down approach with little real empowerment of the workforce. A Continuous Improvement Committee (CIC) was formed and given three projects to work on, rather than letting it identify what it thought was important. Also, the CIC was told that employee development-related projects were not a priority. Finally, the CIC was allowed only to make recommendations to the division lead team (DLT). It was not allowed to implement the improvements it designed, but served only in an advisory role.

The final blow to the empowerment effort came when the division vice president said, "I want quick results," and "Your efforts should not interfere with normal work." He was showing his willingness to sacrifice the employees' quality of working life in order to achieve the desired outcome. Such actions do not demonstrate the respect that is critical to successful efforts. Management in Company X obviously wanted the employees to generate improvements, but to do so without forcing any change in the way things were run. Emphasis remained on making the managers look good, rather than on making the workforce as a whole look good. Once again, the concept of "cultural change" is a concept thrown around by many involved in empowerment efforts, but understood by few.

All employees in Company X were required to attend training sessions. Attendance was monitored and impacted employee performance evaluations. In one division only two trainers existed for nearly one thousand employees spread over a large region. Scheduling the training sessions in this situation was, of course, a major problem. Also, the training was, again, piled on top of their normal workload so that employees resented it.

Training is an important part of any comprehensive empowerment effort. The way it is carried out in most instances, however, is largely a waste of both employee time and company money. Two types of training are involved. The first concerns training on how to function effectively in an empowered environment. This includes training in systems theory, teamwork, facilitation, problem identification and solution, negotiation, and conflict resolution. The second type involves training in technical, rather than social skills. It includes training in areas where the employees will now be making decisions, areas such as customer service, the effective use of computers, the use of machinery, and file keeping.

Company X insisted that everyone participate in empowerment related training up-front. The implication was that adult staff members, most of whom have been employed for a number of years, did not know how to work together effectively, how to identify and solve problems, and how to resolve conflict. The systems approach believes that employees already know most of these things and simply need opportunities to prove it. If there are weaknesses in the way they interact, the weaknesses will be identified and dealt with, or the employees will ask for help. Improvement efforts in a systemic empowerment process, therefore, begin immediately without months of preparatory training.

What Company X covered in terms of technical skills training was, again, defined by management. In the systems approach to empowerment, employees identify a steadily increasing percentage of such training needs. The employees are also given responsibility for designing the involved training sessions, and, whenever possible, for actually delivering the training. But more about that later.

Organization planning at Company X included the identification of organization objectives by top-level executives and the generation of wish lists by lower-level managers. At the onset of this part of the process, executives warned that planning efforts produced work and that those who identified plan-related projects would most likely be given responsibility for running them.

Effective long-range planning is necessary to any successful empowerment process. It provides a frame of reference for problem solving and design efforts; it provides the necessary overview by defining the overall objectives that projects must complement. Long-range planning cannot be done alongside an empowerment process. It must, instead, be a well-integrated part of such processes. Employees must understand and be committed to the organization objectives defined. The best way to develop such understanding and commitment, of course, is to encourage employees on all levels to contribute to the formulation of the objectives.

Having a wish list, similar to the one passed up through the hierarchy at Company X is the workforce going to top management with hat in hand saying, "Please, sir, more por-

ridge..." The wish list approach does not help employees understand the organization's long-range objectives. It does not help units understand each other's operations and how they must fit together. It is antithetical to integration. It encourages competition for resources, rather than the cooperation required for a successful empowerment process. Finally, and perhaps most important to our argument, from the perspective of our standard it encourages unethical behavior.

A LITTLE DAB OF INTRIGUE

As part of the process, employees were asked to complete feedback forms critiquing each other's performance.

Peer evaluations are frequently a cornerstone of the individual-oriented approach to empowerment. Their value is that they sometimes help employees understand each other better; they help clear the air. More frequently, however, they have a negative effect. They breed uncertainty, suspicion, and anger. It is difficult to critique a peer's performance accurately when you do not understand the person's job responsibilities in their entirety, when you do not understand the problems that a person has to deal with, when all you really understand is what happens when you interact with the person. By instituting the peer evaluation approach, Company X further fragmented the process by focusing it on individual performance, rather than on the creation of an atmosphere that encouraged cooperation and teamwork.

When lower-level employees, sometimes through the CIC, *did* make suggestions, managers were reticent to act on them.

Due to the top-down culture found in Company X, and due to the highly competitive atmosphere generated among managers, the question, "Why didn't I think of this before my workers?" was of great concern. "When those working for me identify problems with the way we are currently doing things it makes me look bad in front of my boss. So it is safer to just smother their suggestions."

There is little reason to be surprised that the empowerment process at Company X faded quickly. The rationalization given was that workers on lower levels did not cooperate and did not seem to comprehend the importance of empowerment to the organization and to their own situation. Management also complained that the workers wanted to concentrate on work environment issues. They complained that employees were unwilling to focus instead on issues directly affecting productivity.

A sad, yet familiar ending. Top-level management set the process up for failure by refusing to fully empower those responsible for producing results. Then, it scapegoated them. The fact that workers wanted to deal first with work environment issues—a lack of glare screens, errant drafts from air conditioning vents, a lack of filing cabinet space, telephones that didn't work, and uncomfortable desk chairs—is totally logical in that these issues most immediately affected individual performance.

As a result of these mistakes, in the future, when the next crisis comes and 6-Sigma, or the next popular approach doesn't work, when the executive corps realizes once again that the alternative of real employee empowerment is all it has left, when the executive corps realizes that real employee empowerment is the only approach that makes real sense, getting the workforce involved and committed will be even more difficult.

HOW DO COMPANIES MAKE IT WORK?

Unfortunately, this scenario has been repeated, with variations, time and again at a wide range of companies. The best one can hope for is that it serves as a learning experience and that the next time around management's new understanding will allow a greater degree of success. *The secret is that empowerment will never work, will never produce the desired long-term results until it is full.* How do companies achieve full empowerment? Not only do they need the change in attitude, the change in management culture, the change in management thinking and values that has been discussed at length up to this point, they also need the right approach, the right way to get started.

The two most critical pieces of the *right* approach, of a systemic approach, are the way *training* and the way the involved network of teams are designed. Both pieces are pivotal to every organization improvement effort. Both, however, are usually designed in a non-systemic manner and, therefore, frequently act more as an obstacle to empowerment than as an aid.

We shall finish, therefore, by discussing the way training and team-building need to be organized in order to facilitate true empowerment. Two key questions must be kept in mind during this discussion. First, in terms of training it is necessary to ask, *"Are employees empowered because management has trained them to be so? Or is effective training the result of employees being empowered?"*

Second, because the companies that truly have empowered their work-forces have done so through the appropriate use of teams we must ask, *"Is it possible that the individual can best be empowered through his participation in a team effort? We thought that joining a team took away individual identity and incentive. Does the team approach to individual empowerment really make sense?"*

In Chapter 13, an attempt shall be made to uncover the answers to these questions.

Chapter 13

Training and Teambuilding Make It Work

HOW IT IS NORMALLY DONE

While training is critical to employee empowerment, the traditional training paradigm has been very slow to adapt to modern workplace demands. Without such adaptation, the desired empowerment, as well as the desired bottom line results, likely will not materialize. The training function has traditionally been assigned to the human resources department. The head of training has been totally responsible for the outcome. The development of a training schedule has included the following steps:

- The person in charge of training has participated in the organization's long-range planning effort or has at least been briefed on the long-range objectives generated during that effort.
- This person has afterward either sat down alone or with staff and identified the types of training that should occur during the following year to support the organization's objectives, as well as the resources required to provide this training.
- A schedule has been set, classroom space allocated, time for training negotiated with the heads of the involved departments, and the sessions have begun with either a training department staff member or a consultant presenting the material.

Success has been evaluated in two ways: quantitatively and qualitatively. *Quantitative* measurement judges the success of the process based on the numbers of courses offered and the number of employees who take these courses during the year. *Qualitative* measurement judges success by what is said when participants evaluate the sessions.

This traditional approach is no longer the most effective. Nor is it the most productive in terms of employee empowerment, the bottom line, or improved ethics. The problem is that it does not have the characteristics necessary to make it systemic. One main shortcoming is that it is not truly participative in a systemic sense. Another is that it does little to integrate the various organization functions. A third is that it is usually not ongoing and flexible in a systemic sense. Fourth, a feedback mechanism which allows

117

continuous improvement of the training model might exist (evaluations), but it is not comprehensive. Trainees might say what they believe they are expected to say on evaluations. Or, because the training is forced upon them because they consider it something that must be endured, trainees might see no use in complaining. Or, perhaps, they might not want to alienate the people doing the training.

What we usually end up with in most instances, therefore, is an aggregate of pieces, of individual training sessions strung together without enough attention being paid to the integration of these sessions, to the *whole* that the organization needs to create in terms of training. What we end up with is training delivered to employees who frequently do not understand why they are receiving it.

THE SYSTEMS APPROACH TO TRAINING

Let us go over the characteristics necessary to a systemic training effort one at a time. *First is participativeness.* Most trainers consider their sessions to be participative. Employees are frequently involved in hands-on exercises. They break down into groups and practice a problem-solving technique, a creativity enhancing technique, a statistical measurement technique. They role-play and sharpen their conflict resolution skills. They take part in discussions on organization ethics. They actually work with a new piece of equipment. From a systems perspective, however, such activities result, once again, in only *partial participation* and do not produce the best results.

The classes and exercises themselves are not where participation needs to begin in order to produce the best overall results. Instead, participation needs to begin at the beginning. To be most effective participation needs to begin when the types of training to be delivered are identified. Once long-term organization objectives are defined during a planning process, top-level management usually thinks it has a pretty good idea of what new skills need to be learned and of what old skills need to be updated. But managers, while defining these training needs are doing so with a top-down rather than a bottom-up perspective. Their reaction to or their interpretation of a unit's situation is usually quite different from that of the people actually in the trenches, actually doing the work and actually dealing with process-related problems. It is the employees behind the desk or operating the machine who understand best what is wrong with the work flow, who understand why coworkers are having trouble meeting deadlines and why customers are complaining about the response they get when calling to place an order.

To be participative in a systemic sense and, therefore, to be truly empowering, the training paradigm *must encourage the involvement of lower-level workers, as well as managers in the definition of training needs.* It must also, when possible, allow employees to contribute to the design of training modules. Finally, when realistic, it should encourage workers to actually help deliver the training.

From a systems perspective, therefore, we realize that participation must be incorporated into every phase of the training paradigm, not just the delivery phase and not just peripherally. An additional major benefit of adopting such an approach is that it takes a great deal of the pressure off the manager in charge of training. By making the paradigm truly participative, everybody shares the responsibility and everybody functions as a check on the usefulness of the training delivered. The head of training, in this instance, becomes a facilitator, assisting the efforts of employees on all levels to identify and to meet their own training needs, which, if we are talking about *learning* rather than *teaching*, should have been one of her roles from the start.

In terms of the second systems characteristic the need for *integration* of training efforts across the entire organization, most companies again fall short. They do so because the definition of training needs usually comes *after* long-range objectives have been identified, rather than as part of that process. The possibility of providing employees with the training necessary to meet objectives is not usually a consideration during strategic planning sessions. A majority of companies also fall short in terms of integration because staff training is not a top priority for most managers. It is fitted into the most convenient schedule slot, allowing little coordination in terms of what is being offered in different parts of the organization.

When the systems perspective is adopted, a vehicle, usually a network of teams, is created that allows representatives from all units to meet periodically, not only to identify training needs, but also to schedule sessions in a way that makes sense. Such a team structure and such meetings help ensure that the organization's effort is ongoing and flexible. When representatives from the various departments sit down together, such things as unexpected operational changes are discussed, allowing ramifications to be understood more rapidly on a company-wide rather than just a unit-wide basis. Also, during such meetings the training agenda is reviewed and modified.

This flexibility, of course, as well as the increased participation and integration put more pressure on the training department. In our new scenario, however, the training function is no longer just three or four people struggling to meet the growing demands of upper-level management. Rather, it is a well-integrated, organization-wide network of individuals representing all functions who share the involved responsibilities.

Finally, the feedback that encourages continual learning, as well as continual improvement of the training model is a given when the systems approach is adopted and a team network created.

A COMPANY THAT GREW TOO RAPIDLY

Perhaps the best way to bring the systems model of training to life is to present a case history of a company that adopted it. Company Y is a young, aggressive investor in the non-conforming mortgage market. It is in the business of originating, purchasing, selling, and servicing home equity loans to borrowers whose financial needs may not be met by traditional financial institutions.

In 1992, this company employed approximately 50 full-time employees. By the end of 1995, that number had grown to approximately 420 full-time employees. In early 1996, the parent firm became publicly held, which meant that Company Y gained access to more resources and could service a higher volume of accounts. By September of 1996, the company employed 500 people in its home and field offices.

One serious result of this rapid growth was the need to upgrade the computer support system. Originally, new employees required few or no computer skills to fill data-processing positions. Much of the work was done by hand. Now, however, due to rapidly increasing volume, the decision was made to upgrade the main computer system and to provide the necessary training for those who did the work.

Previously, Company Y had trained without the benefit of a formal program. Previously, employees had learned most of their skills on the job. Process and technical changes were passed along by word-of-mouth. This meant that both the quantity and the quality of the training received were haphazard. In addition, while some units had begun documenting the policies and procedures that applied to their part of the operation, no organization-wide policies and procedures existed. Each unit did its own thing. While this approach had sufficed when the company was small, it became increasingly ineffective as Company Y grew.

In May of 1996, a training coordinator was hired to design and implement a company-wide training program. Much latitude was given. The coordinator was, in effect, offered a *greenfield site* opportunity. Her responsibilities included the training of new employees, the updating of long-term employees' skills and the preparation of associates for managerial positions. In addition, due to the pressures resulting from the rapid changes occurring, the coordinator was asked to address stress related issues.

A complication was that traditional sources of assistance—external consultants, off-the-shelf training programs, etc.—would not be available. The budget was already in place for the fiscal year and no funds had been allocated for such things. A second complication was that, being a one-person department, the training coordinator could not possibly design and deliver all the required training herself.

The only alternative available at that point was to utilize resources currently possessed by the company. Adopting a systems perspective, the coordinator formed a team composed of supervisors representing every unit of Company Y. Initially, the team met three times a month for one hour. Members identified four levels of training needs. The first level included the training needs of each team member's own unit. The second level included types of training requested by more than one unit. The third included organization-wide training needs. The fourth included various types of training that team members thought might be beneficial for clients. Prioritization of the training needs identified was based on a review of corporate objectives with representatives of upper-level management participating.

Team members were responsible for acting as a liaison between the training team and their individual units, for bringing to the meetings issues important to their units, and for reporting back to their units the decisions made. Added to this, training team members, whenever possible, were responsible for the design and the delivery of the actual training modules. The training coordinator's main role was to support team members in their efforts and to help integrate the desired whole. Top-level management was invited to team meetings on an as-needed basis to provide input concerning changing organization priories. In addition, top-level management was asked to approve written training materials before they were distributed.

SAMPLE TRAINING TEAM PROJECTS

The training team's first project was development of an *Employee Orientation Program*. Each member provided an outline, from his perspective, of the main training points to be covered for new employees. The training coordinator then combined these outlines into the beginning of an employee manual that could be used during orientation presentations. Access to this document would also enable team members to train ongoing associates who showed a weakness or who asked for assistance.

Next, the training team refined the actual orientation presentation, building in the flexibility necessary to deal with the range of expertise new employees needed to acquire. Eventually, this project produced a design for a week-long training session that encompassed everything from an introduction complete with new-hire paperwork and a tour of the facilities, to technology training, to a study of policies and procedures, to workbook exercises. At the end of each week-long session, new associates were surveyed and asked what they would add or change. A second survey was sent both to employees and their supervisors after one year on the job. It assessed changes in their skill levels since orientation. Results of this survey provided input that contributed to the design of advanced and more specific training modules.

The third project undertaken by the training team was development of a *client user guide* and a *client quick reference aid*. The team thought that by pre-training potential customers concerning what the company would purchase, the buying-selling process would be expedited and overall communications improved. Also, through a joint effort with members of the sales force an annual survey was developed and sent out to uncover additional customer needs. Once survey results were analyzed, the training team met to address the concerns posed by customers and to begin brainstorming training-related solutions.

In summation, the Company Y training effort was shaped to be participative in the broad sense, to be organization-wide and integrated, to be ongoing, and to ensure the opportunity for continual feedback from all directions including the customer. This happened because the new training coordinator, when faced with an unusual situation, chose to think systemically. Instead of becoming a "Lone Ranger," she became a facilitator, and by so doing, with the necessary support from upper-level management, helped create a situation that has greatly reduced the possibility of failure, both in terms of fulfilling her individual responsibilities and in terms of Company Y meeting its overall business objectives.

THE TEAM APPROACH AS THE SECOND VEHICLE NECESSARY TO EMPOWERMENT

Company Y could not have developed its successful and relatively inexpensive approach to training without the formation of a *training team*. We are going to elaborate now on the belief that team efforts are critical, not only to systemic training but to any attempt at effective, organization-wide empowerment.

Of course, everybody knows that individual efforts are important as well. Everybody knows of people who have individually come up with and have taken the lead in developing revolutionary new ideas. This is one of the things that empowerment is about. This is one of the foundational underpinnings of our economy. Thus, Henry Ford developed the concept of the gasoline-powered engine and revolutionized assembly-line production. Thus, in modern times, Bill Gates developed a product, as well as a marketing strategy that allowed him to dominate the computer industry.

But even the most brilliant entrepreneurs realize they can't do it all by themselves. They realize that once past the idea stage they need to bring in others with expertise in production, marketing, finance, and, as the organization grows, human resources. Smart industrial leaders have also realized that one good idea no longer suffices. Copies or even improved copies appear very quickly to compete. The key is no longer just one good idea, but continuous improvement, and continuous improvement on any scale requires a well-integrated organization where information flows freely, where people have immediate access to what they need, and where ideas circulate quickly and receive enrichment from all quarters and perspectives.

The vehicle best suited to encourage this type of environment is the team. The team allows companies to elicit, channel, and integrate the contributions of employees in the most effective manner. From the employees' perspective, the team allows individual ideas to be tested and improved upon by peers. The downside of this approach is that individuals can no longer take full credit for their idea. The upside is that they can take credit for their contribution to a wide range of ideas and, unless they are Henry Ford or Bill Gates, can benefit more in the long run. In terms of integration, a correctly designed team approach makes it possible for ideas and projects to feed off each other, creating a final result that is "more than the sum of its parts."

Once again, most organizations serious about effectively utilizing employee potential say they have a team approach in place. But, once again, most team approaches empower members only partially so that only partial use is made of their potential.

THREE FOUNDATIONAL TYPES OF TEAMS

Three types of teams have traditionally been used in empowerment efforts. Unfortunately, the type that empowers the least has been used the most. This is the *task force*. A majority of employees are, at some point, asked to participate in a task force effort. A project is defined by management. A cross-functional group of employees possessing the necessary skills is brought together and led by the highest-level manager involved. Group members are responsible for clarifying the involved issues, defining the best approach, and making recommendations to the person or people who formed the task force. When their assignment is completed, the team is disbanded. A task force, therefore, is top-down driven, problem specific, and allowed only to make recommendations. It has nothing to do with identifying the problem to be worked on, the implementation of the solution decided upon, or with monitoring the results of the involved changes.

The task force is, indeed, a useful vehicle for designing organization improvements. It has proven its value. But in terms of maximizing the utilization of team member potential, it is the weakest alternative. Employees are told what to work on. They enjoy a brief moment in the sun when they are encouraged to bring their intelligence and experience to bear on the design of a solution. But that's it. Afterward, the learning curve crashes. They are not usually allowed to try their solution out or to fine-tune it.

The second type of team is a product of the quality improvement movement. It can be called an *ongoing improvement team*. An integrated network of these teams representing all organization functions and levels is formed. The teams meet regularly to identify improvements that members think necessary, to design those improvements, and then to take the lead in implementing and fine-tuning them.

This is full empowerment. No one is allowed to tell the teams what to work on. At the same time, all team members have to obey a set of process ground rules established to make sure they have access to desired resources and to protect them from those against empowerment. These rules also ensure that team efforts complement, rather than contradict organization objectives, and ensure that the efforts are integrated.

Ground rules for fully empowered teams include the following:

1. *Teams have access to all company personnel to meet their informational needs.*
   The best way to starve a team-driven empowerment effort is to withhold information team members need for projects. This is exactly what those against empowerment do.

2. *Response to team questions and project ideas must be received within one week. The response to project ideas can be, "Yes, go ahead with it," "No, and this is why," with a reasonable explanation, or "Let's talk," with a date set.*
   Even though team members are assured access to all company personnel for informational purposes, those approached can stall. This is another, more subtle way of sabotaging empowerment efforts. Ground rule number two makes such stalling impossible.

3. *Teams must meet, at least initially, on a regular basis and members must be allowed to attend meetings.*
   Another good way of blocking an empowerment effort is to say, "Sorry, but my workers are too busy today to attend the meeting." If this strategy succeeds once, if one manager is allowed to get away with it, the strategy will be used over and over and will spread throughout the organization, leading, eventually, to the disbanding of teams. Meeting time must be protected.

4. *When a ground rule is violated, the team facilitator will meet with the violator for resolution. If the problem is not overcome, the facilitator will report the violation to the head facilitator who coordinates the facilitator network. If the head facilitator cannot resolve the issue she will carry it to top-level management.*
   Ground rules are useless unless a "hammer" exists, unless someone with real power over those who would break them is willing to intercede and keep such people from doing so. Ground rule number three sets up the necessary "hammer" if top-level management is willing to play its role when the head facilitator asks for help.

5. *Improvements and projects that might affect other parts of the operation must be agreed to by anyone else affected before implementation. These stakeholders must also be given a chance to contribute to the design.*
   This is the other side of the coin. Teams cannot go around making any changes they want. Forcing teams to involve others who will be affected turns an improvement process into a learning process as well. Team members learn how what they do, or what they want to do, will affect others. It also helps to integrate the effort.

6. *Team-suggested improvements must be justified by a cost-benefit analysis when possible or by a quality of working life rationale when not possible.*
   When team members do a cost-benefit analysis they begin to understand the tie between their ideas and the bottom line. They also learn more about organization budgeting and about how organization priorities are set. A quality of working life rationale is used when things

cannot be quantified. It explains the indirect benefit of the desired change. Examples would be putting glare screens on computers or getting rid of drafts.

So now time has been set aside to work on projects. Team members and their ideas are protected. Access to desired information is assured. The integration of team efforts throughout the organization is forced. But, in fact, do these ground rules ensure full empowerment?

Not really.

If the individual teams in the network are structured the way most team are structured, the way task forces, for example, are structured, if hourly or professional workers are combined with managers, the empowerment will, once again, be only partial at best. The managers involved will take the lead in identifying what to work on. They will take the lead in the design process. They will take the lead in the identification and enactment of implementation steps. They might encourage others to contribute, to talk, but everyone will look to *them*, everyone will listen carefully to what *they* say when decision time comes.

It is very hard for workers to accept the declaration that, "During normal working hours what I say goes, but during this one hour a week when the improvement teams meets we will all be equals, decisions will be made by consensus." It is a difficult line to swallow, no matter how sincere the manager might be. The boss is still the boss.

With this critical issue in mind, there is one other characteristic of the systems approach to team building that makes *all the difference in the world* when we are talking about empowerment. It is the characteristic that scares most companies away from the systems model, but it is absolutely necessary. Quite simply, *hourly or professional employees do not sit on the same teams as managers*. That is it. That is the last key to full empowerment. Hourly workers have their own teams defined by function. Managers have their own teams defined either by function or by level of management. Hourly workers and managers are not mixed.

Immediately the cry goes up, "But how do you keep the hourly teams under control? How do you keep them from making mistakes due to their lack of expertise or perspective? How do you keep them from wasting time?" The answer is, of course, the *ground rules*. It is inevitable that a manager is going to be affected by any team-proposed change. Therefore, managers will necessarily be asked for their input.

But isn't this getting back to business as usual? No, it is not. *A very big difference exists between having managers sitting on teams as members and inviting them to attend meetings on an as-needed basis*. In the latter case the workers are in control. They have identified the project they want to work on. They have designed the solution or are in the process of designing the solution. The manager is called in simply to provide necessary information or to offer an opinion. Then he leaves. Although the manager's agreement is necessary before the desired change can be made, that person is not running the show.

And if the manager makes objections she must explain why and work with team members to achieve an acceptable alternative. If the manager becomes insistent and unreasonable, team members, through their facilitator and the "hammer" ground rule, can seek support elsewhere.

But managers rarely do make unreasonable objections. They learn very quickly the value of this arrangement. Not having to make every decision and not having to oversee the activities of the hourly teams frees up large amounts of time. Managers can now work on the projects *they* think important because management-level teams are also empowered by the ground rules, their efforts are also protected from those above who might feel threatened.

The third type of empowering team is *the self-directed work group*, a concept that seems to be gaining steadily in popularity. While the *ongoing improvement team* focuses on improving products, manufacturing and service processes, management systems, and the work environment, while the *task force* is project specific and, therefore, not ongoing, *the self-directed work group* is responsible for a unit's day-to-day operations, for meeting the unit's day-to-day production goals.

Basically, this team approach can be called, "*Doing what you were hired to do but without managers.*" The authority and responsibility traditionally held by managers have been taken over by the workers themselves. Self-directed work groups decide who will do what job. They set their own schedules, solve their own problems, and sometimes even hire and fire. The manager's role in this environment is to contribute when called upon for assistance and to help integrate that section's efforts with what is going on in the rest of the organization. Self-directed work groups allow the full empowerment of members, at least in their own area of expertise.

TYING IT ALL TOGETHER

It should be fairly obvious that in terms of these three types of empowering teams we do not have an "either-or" situation. While each type can stand alone, they also can be combined. When all three are used, the self-directed work groups are in charge of daily operation and of meeting unit production requirements; the ongoing improvement teams meet periodically to identify, design, and implement positive changes; and task forces can be formed at any time, usually to deal with issues involving more than one unit or to deal with issues identified by management that no improvement team is currently addressing.

One other type of empowering team that ties things together has been designed by Russell Ackoff. In his model each manager in the organization has a *board*. On this board sit the manager, her boss, and her direct reports. The board is responsible for planning the efforts of that unit, for setting unit policy, for coordinating the efforts of those reporting to the manager, for integrating the efforts of the manager's unit with those above and those below (which is facilitated by the fact that the manager's boss sits on *his* boss's board and by the fact that the manager's reports sit on *their* reports' boards), for evaluating the performance of the manager whose board it is, and for taking the lead in making improvements in unit products, manufacturing or service processes, and work environment. Such boards can obviously create task forces.

This "circular organization" model is perhaps the ultimate in empowerment because it gives employees control not only over their work environment, *but also over their leaders*. None of the other empowering team arrangements possess this characteristic. Boards in a *circular organization* lack the authority to fire the manager whose board it is, but members can decide the person is not qualified to continue in that position and must look elsewhere in the company for employment.

So, *training* and *team building* are the two major vehicles for empowering employees. And, of course, these two vehicles support each other. One of the major activities of empowered team members in a systemic operation is the identification, the design, and the delivery of desired training. Looking in the other direction, a great deal of training is necessary for team-empowered employees to function effectively. They need to understand their responsibilities and the responsibilities of their peers. They need to understand how to use their new authority to integrate efforts in their unit. They need to understand how to integrate the efforts of their unit with those of other units. They need to understand how what their unit does fits into the organization's operation as a whole and how their budget fits into the organization's budget as a whole.

Finally, in terms of ethics, as has been said several times, when employees are empowered, when they have control over their work lives, when their contributions are recognized, when their reward is tied to their productivity and they are assisted by the company in efforts to improve that productivity, there is much less reason for unethical behavior.

At the same time, when people are well-trained and work in teams, when key information is not hidden away but made available to everyone, when decisions are arrived at in an open manner with all those affected being encouraged to contribute directly or indirectly, and when an evaluation and reward system is used that encourages employees to support each other's efforts, an evaluation and reward system that says at the same time, "If you are doing something unethical and I don't stop you or get the team to stop you, I'm going to be hurt as well as the company," there is much less chance of unethical behavior occurring.

Also there is much more rapid progress toward the realization of our idealized ethical meta-standard.

Bibliography

Ackoff, Russell, *The Democratic Corporation*, New York: Oxford University Press, 1994.

Ackoff, Russell and Emery, Fred, *On Purposeful Systems*, New York: Aldine-Atherton, 1972.

Bielski, Vince, Our Magnificent Obsession, *The Family Therapy Networker*, March/April 1996.

Churchman, C. West, *The Systems Approach*, New York: Dell Publishing Co., 1968.

Churchman, C. West and Ackoff, Russell, *Methods of Inquiry: An Introduction to Philosophy and Scientific Methods*, St. Lewis: Educational Publishers, 1950.

Cole, Margaret, *Robert Owen of New Lanark*, New York: Oxford University Press, 1953.

Devine, Philip, *Relativism, Nihilism, and God*, Notre Dame, Indiana: University of Notre Dame Press, 1989.

Dunlap, Albert, *Mean Business*, New York: Random House, 1996.

Elliot, Ronald "The Challenge of Managing Change," *Personnel Journal*, March, 1990, 39.

"Few Recover Totally from Downsizing," *USA Today*, August 1998.

Fuller, Tom, "Does Business Need Leaders?" *Business Horizons*, July/August 1995.

Gelderman, Carol, *Henry Ford: The Wayward Capitalist*, New York: The Dial Press, 1981.

Gharajedaghi, Jamshid, *Systems Thinking: Managing Chaos and Complexity*, Boston: Butterworth & Heinemann, 1999.

Henkoff, Ronald "Cost Cutting: How to Do It Right." *Fortune*, April 1990.

James, William, *Pragmatism and Four Essays on the Meaning of Truth*, New York: Meridian Books, 1959.

Jean-Paul Sartre, *The Age of Reason*, New York: Bantam Books, 1964.

Josephson, Martin, *The Robber Barons: The Great American Capitalists*, New York: Harcourt Brace & Co. 1934.

Lacy, Robert, *Ford: The Men and the Machine*, Boston: Little Brown, 1986.

Laszlo, Ervin, *The Systems View of the World: The Natural Philosophy of the New Developments in the Sciences*, New York: George Braziller, 1972.

Levering, Robert and Moshowitz, Milton, *100 Best Companies to Work For in America*, New York: Penguin Group, 1994.

Machiavelli, Niccole, *The Prince*, New York: Barnes and Noble, 1994.

Maslow, Abraham, *Motivation and Personality*, New York: Harper and Row, 1970.

Mill, John Stuart, *Autobiography*, New York: Bobbs-Merrill, 1957.

Mill: Utilitarianism: With Critical Essays, ed. Samuel Gorowitz, New York: The Bobbs-Merrill Co. Inc., 1971.

Morris, Tom, *If Aristotle Ran General Motors*, New York: Holt, Rinehart Co. 1997.

Nietzche, Frederick Wilhelm, *Thus Spoke Zarathustra*, New York: Modern Library, 1995.

"No Bosses and Even Leaders Can't Give Orders," *Business Week*, Oct. 12, 1990.

Novak, Michael, *The Experience of Nothingness*, New York: Harper and Row, 1970.

Petrick, Joseph and Quinn, John, *Management Ethics: Integrity at Work*, Sage Publications, 1997.

Reynolds Fisher, Susan, "Downsizing in a Learning Organization: Are There Hidden Costs?" *Academy of Management Review*, Jan. 2000.

Roth, William, "The Dangerous Ploy of Downsizing," *Business Forum*, Fall, 1993.

Roth, "Dealing With the Corporate Hotdogs," *The Journal for Quality and Participation*, Fall, 2000.

Roth, "The End of Performance Appraisals?" *Quality Digest*, September 1944.

Roth, "Going All the Way With Empowerment," *The TQM Magazine*, Vol. 9, No.1, 1997.

Roth, *Quality Improvement: A Systems Perspective*, Delray Beach, Florida, St. Lucie Press, 1999.

Roth, *The Roots and Future of Management Theory: A Systems Perspective*, Delray Beach, Florida: St. Lucie Press, 2000.

Roth, "Work Ethic," *National Productivity Review*, Autumn 1998.

Roth, William & Klopp, Sharon, "In the New World Traditional Training Hurts the Bottom Line," *Journal for Quality and Participation*, June, 1997.

Roth, William & Potts, Marjorie, "Doing It Wrong: A Case Study" *Quality Progress*, February, 2001.

Schon, Donald, *Beyond the Stable State*, New York: W.W. Norton & Co., 1971.

Seife, Charles, *Zero: The Biography of a Dangerous Idea*, New York: Penguin Books, 2000.

Semler, Ricardo, "Managing Without Managers," *Harvard Business Review*, September-October 1989.

Slutsker, Gary, "Hog Wild," *Forbes*, May 24, 1993.

Smith, Huston, *The Religions of Man*, New York: Harper and Row 1958.

"So What's So Great About Norway?" *The Philadelphia Inquirer*, November 25, 2001.

Stayer, Ralph, "How I Learned to Let My Workers Lead," *Harvard Business Review*, November-December 1990.

Stayer, Ralph, "Managing the Journey," *INC.*, November 1990.

Systems Thinking, ed. Fred Emery, New York: Penguin Education, 1976.

"The Corporate Elite," *Business Week*, October 1989.

The Downsizing of America, Created by The New York Times, New York: Random House, 1969.

The Koran, translated by N.J. Dawood, Baltimore: Penguin Books, 1959.

Velasquez, Manuel, *Business Ethics*, 4th edition, Saddle River, N.J.: Prentice Hall, 1998.

Vinacke, Edgar, *Foundations of Psychology*, New York: American Book Co. 1968.

"World-Class Workaholics," *U.S. News and World Report*, Dec. 20, 1999.

"World of Work," *The Magazine of the International Labor Organization*, No. 31, September/October 1999.

References

Chapter 1
1. "Sunbeam Board in Revolt, Ousts Job-Cutting Chairman" *New York Times*, June 16, 1998, p. A1.
2. Dunlap, Albert and Bob Andelman. *Mean Business*. (New York: Times Business, 1996), pp. 197–199.

Chapter 3
1. Josephson, Martin. *Robber Barons: The Great American Capitalist*. (New York: Harcourt Brace & Co., 1934) p. 7.
2. Ibid., p. 29.

Chapter 4
1. "Keep Your Profits," *Newsweek*, November 1995, p. 98.
2. Josephson, *Robber Barons*, p. 441.
3. Ibid., p. 18, 19.

Chapter 9
1. Vinacke, Edgar. *Foundations of Psychology*. (New York: American Book Co., 1968), p. 389.
2. Maslow, Abraham H. *Motivation and Personality*. (New York: Harper and Row, 1970), p. 45.

Index

RECEIVED

RECEIVED

~ 3 OCT 2012